Ayelet Porat

THE JOY
OF BEING ME

Self-Awareness for a Better Life

Book 1

Professional advisor: Amit Offir

Editor: Sharon Moldaver

Cover and book design: Studio Lev Ari

Best Seller
Books

Ayelet Porat

THE JOY OF BEING ME

Self-Awareness for a Better Life

Book 1

Know, Accept and Love Yourself
Be the person you always wanted to be!

Table of Contents:

Introduction

About the author

Ayelet Porat is **a research psychologist (M.A)** and is a **certified facilitator of self-awareness groups** and personal empowerment processes. She has also specialized in some alternative medicine fields: **Reflexology, Bach Flowers Remedies, Reiki** (Master-Teacher degree) and more. She has been involved in these fields for **over twenty years**. The combination of the different fields enables her to understand the beauty and power inherent in working with the body, soul and spirit.

She imparts the vast knowledge she has accumulated as **a lecturer, a therapist, a workshop facilitator** and **an author.**

Ayelet has published **eight books,** which have already helped thousands of people to change their lives. At the present time, Ayelet is working on her next book and she continues exploring the vast **field of self-awareness** in order to share more of her expertise with her followers and readers around the globe.

Why is it important to adopt self-awareness as a way of life?

Hello!

This book can change your life, as it will open for you a vast and wonderful world of life with self-awareness, both practical and spiritual!

Self-awareness is a way of life that aspires, first of all, to bring a person who chooses it to know, accept and love himself. This is very important because when we are feeling good we are much stronger and more able to function in an efficient and beneficial way in the society in which we live. In addition, we have an empowered ability to create a good life for ourselves, in which we have an endless supply of energy and joy and we know where we are headed. We can create for ourselves a reality in which we express our abilities and desires, fulfill our dreams and realize our destiny. **In short, self-awareness is a way of life in which we are happier!**

I have been professionally involved in this field for more than twenty years, but in fact, self-awareness has been an inseparable part of my life since my early childhood.

Already as a very young girl I could recognize when things were not good for me and I found ways of thinking and functional strategies to improve my feelings. Over the years I developed methods to alleviate my heartaches, to function more successfully as part of the society in which I grew up and to change within myself what I understood needed changing. Only at a much later stage did I discover that my lifestyle was called "Self-Awareness."

Everything I have learned over the years I pass on through my books, in personal training and guidance, as well as in courses and workshops. **I believe in the human spirit and in the amazing ability that we all have, to create for ourselves a wonderful life. My ambition is to help each person help themselves! This guide certainly seeks to bring to the world a way of life which is rich and full of happiness.**

At this point I would like to say a few words about spirituality. Self-awareness is essentially a work of improvement and a way to effect changes in ourselves. These are very practical changes in thought, emotion and behavior and altering habits which do not serve us well. We want to take control of our patterns so they do not continue to manage us automatically. We want the ability to choose how we experience, interpret and run our daily reality. **This is a very practical form of self-awareness. However, we are also spiritual beings and it is advisable to include the spiritual part in the creation of our current reality.** This book refers to that in detail, since I see each person as a physical and spiritual being, an entity composed of body, soul and spirit. It is possible that you, the reader, do not believe in God or in any other supreme power. It is also possible that you do not think that we have an eternal spirit that comes from God. That is fine. This book will benefit you as well and I suggest reading it with an open mind and taking from it whatever suits you!

How to get the best out of this book

This book is the first part of the self-awareness courses guide and has a follow-up book with advanced courses. It is recommended to start with this book and upon finishing it, go on to Book #2: "Freedom, Abundance and Fulfillment".

Most of the chapters contain exercises to help you apply the material. You can practice immediately at the end of each chapter. Alternatively, you can read the whole book, then return to each chapter separately to perform the exercises.

I highly recommend performing the exercises, since there is a big difference between reading and learning new principles, and actually applying them. After all, you are reading this book to improve your life, not just reading it in the theory! Buy a beautiful notebook that will inspire you to write, thereby ensuring that you will complete the exercises.

Important Note

The book is written as a guide for students who are considering enrolling in practical and spiritual self-awareness studies at the Faculty of Good Life Sciences. Each chapter of the book describes one course in the curriculum of the faculty and is an introduction to one subject in self-awareness. **After reading both parts of the guide (Book #1 and Book #2) you will have a complete picture of the subject. You will have a deep understanding of what self-awareness is and how it is expressed on a daily basis in the life of a person who has decided to adopt it as a way of life.**

The chapters in the book are written using both male and female allusions and examples. This is due to my desire to include both sexes equally and also with the understanding that each of us has both a masculine and a feminine side.

I wish you enjoyable and enriching reading and I am sure that already during reading the book/s you will feel your life changing for the better.

Lovingly,

At your service always,

Ayelet Porat

Head of the Department for Practical and Spiritual Self-Awareness

The Faculty of Good Life Sciences

Let's get started!

The Self-Awareness Path

Congratulations!

Greetings on reaching the decision to check whether you should begin to study self-awareness. Please be warned that you are about to explore a path that begins now and ends only when life is over. If you commit to this path, it is a lifelong commitment.

Let me rephrase. You had better be ready for a serious addiction. Because when you begin to understand why you chose this path, **you will never want to leave!**

I must tell you beforehand that you will not receive any certificate, medal, award or degree attesting to your study achievements. There is no tangible sign and there is no scholarship ceremony for outstanding students. This is not so bad, because there are great results to be achieved and that is what matters. True, you will not enter the great pantheon of self-awareness, because there is no such thing, **but you will be much happier!** Your life will improve dramatically, your relationships with yourself and with others will become more fulfilling, and happiness will become a more familiar and everyday experience for you.

OK. What do these studies require of you? What will the self-awareness course ask you to do?

Let me explain.

First, **the contract you sign is with yourself, only**. You have no obligation to the institution where the studies take place. By the way, I like to call this institution "Life", "The Universe", "The University of Good Life" or "The place to figure out who I am, where I came from and where I'm going". Choose whichever name you like best ☺

As I stated, your contract is only with yourself. That is fine but if you fear that without supervision you simply will not persevere, that is a justifiable concern. Not everyone has sufficient self-discipline. If this is the case, you should appoint a supervisor. Someone who will commit and who will see that you follow your curriculum. It can be a good friend, a responsible relative, or one of your faculty teachers.

You will learn how to identify and dismantle accumulated loads that block you in many ways, to change thought patterns and fine-tune your choices. **You can apply all the methods to yourself only**. You have no right or permission to try to change anyone else. This is a very important point in self-awareness. We will teach you a wide range of skills but they are for your own use only. If another person wants to imitate you, that is their business. If someone wishes to use you as an example, they can as long as it is their choice. If you are asked to share what you know or teach someone - only then will you be free to share your knowledge with them.

In other words, the fact that you start learning and advancing through the stages of self-awareness does not give you the status of a guru. You will not become a missionary nor a mentor or earn the title of a teacher or a preacher. I hope this point is clear. **You have no mandate to change anyone except yourself.**

This is true in any situation. Even if you have children. The only way to teach them what you will learn here is by setting a personal example. As you improve yourself, they may choose to follow you. You should not try to change them. Maybe when your children grow up, they will buy this guide and come to study with us. However, this of course will be their choice ☺

Another important point you should know before you commit: **it will not always be a pleasant ride.** At times, you will have to face fear, pain, anger, hate and other unpleasant feelings that are buried within you. On other occasions you will meet parts of yourself that you rather would not have. The same goes for events you would prefer to forget. You will find yourself passing through torrential rivers of sorrow, crossing the dark forests of the soul and confronting demons and monsters, some of whom you have created yourself. You will need to treat old wounds and ugly scars. Sometimes you will have to look in the mirror, realize that you have many faces and that not all are beautiful, but nonetheless are part of the collection that is you! Therefore, as stated, it will not always be a pleasant journey. But, (and here I am happy to say there is a "but") from my experience I can tell you that you get used to it, **you even begin to enjoy the adventures of the journey into yourself,** with all its surprises, including the less pleasant ones.

Are you still willing to consider reading this guide further? I warn you again, when you begin this journey there is no turning back. Do you want to know what else is required of you? Let me see...

The self-aware person relinquishes a large part of his personality, especially the ego. **He agrees to change.** This may be obvious to you, but maybe we should take a moment to think about this. You may have bought this guide precisely because you want to change! However, I'm not sure you understood the implications of the whole process. As a self-awareness student, **you will be required to give up your self-importance.** One of the recommendations in this study course is to constantly tell yourself that you are not important. Try it: "I am not important!" How does it feel?

Let me reassure you that you **are** important, but no more important than anyone else. The point is, if you remember that you do not matter, that the story is not about you, that you are not the center of the world, life will become a lot simpler. You will not be hurt by anything, you will not be offended, you will expect less and therefore you will be less disappointed. In general, this will make it much easier for you to become a student of self-awareness. Self-importance is an excess load you will not need once you begin to acquire healthy self-awareness.

The self-change you agree to undergo has consequences, sometimes there is a price to pay. First of all, **it is rather difficult to sustain change.** We tend to revert to old habits. In other words, it is a stubborn war and one needs to develop willpower. Think of it as subscribing to a gym with a goal to develop a will of iron. Obviously, self-discipline and the ability to persevere in training on almost a daily basis are required. The good news is that after a period of about 21 days new habits tend to replace the old ones. Sometimes this period can take 40 days but that is still reasonable. In very special cases there is a need for more determined persistence, but by the time you encounter such cases, you will already have acquired the knowledge required and this will not be a problem for you. You will be able to help yourself with a vast array of tools.

You will find that self-transformation will have another side effect. **Not everyone will love the fact that you are changing!** I will risk saying there will even be people who will get mad at you and may try to sabotage your progress. Their motives will vary from jealousy, through the fear of losing you, to the fact that you will be a mirror in which they will have to see where they themselves have to change. Your changing may cause the people who surround you great discomfort and unpleasant feelings and they will not thank you for that.

As a result, there is another possible implication of the changes that will occur: you may **lose friends. There will be periods in which you will find that you are pretty lonely.** You see, when you start to take more responsibility for yourself and for your life and start to change, some old friends will suddenly no longer fit in your life. You may find them boring or vice versa. You will no longer share the same interests; you may urge them to share in all your newfound knowledge, but they may not be receptive. You will realize that some friends are unsuitable and that your friendship with them is really not good for you. You may find that you meet up with them less often. Do not worry. **Soon you will begin to make new friends**. They will be friends that accompany you on the journey to self-awareness and are going through exactly the same process as you. Whether they are beginners or veterans, you will enjoy their company and they will enjoy yours. Together you will delve into the wide world of self-awareness. Furthermore, there is another good thing that will happen to you. You will begin to realize that, even if there is no one beside you, you are never alone. This is not the place to expand on this point, so for now you will just have to believe me.

Before you start reading the guide, I want to point out something very important. There is such a thing as "over-awareness" meaning too much "digging", which is no longer a positive thing. I mentioned before that you need to take into account that you get addicted to it, remember? So, at times, it is necessary to take complete breaks from the studies and the implementation of the materials being studied. You are being required, as an aware person, to look at yourself and at your thoughts, feelings and actions through a magnifying glass. What am I saying? Sometimes you are required to virtually place everything under the lens of a microscope! This can be very tiring and can even cause visual distortions and unclear perceptions. There have been cases where students totally lost it, they forgot who they were, they forgot what the whole thing was about and they did not stop "digging". They drove themselves and everyone else crazy. It became unbearable. We had to seek medical help for them and required them to stop studying in order to help them restore balance.

I will give you one basic rule before you start reading the guide. The rule is: **you are perfect as you are here and now**. Do you get this? **You are perfect as you are here and now!** If you decide to enroll in these studies and commit yourself to a path of self-awareness, I must warn you: **do not forget to take vital breaks and just be!**

That is it, I have said what I needed to say. You are now invited to set off on your journey. In the following chapters, you will find a list of the various courses offered by the Faculty of Practical and Spiritual Self-Awareness. Take time to read each chapter thoroughly. Choose exercises from the wide range that the guide offers you, so that at the end you will have a clear picture of all the topics studied. Needless to say, I shall be delighted to meet with you again, after you have read the entire guide, when you come to register for our courses.

Goodbye and good luck!

Ayelet Porat

Head of the Department for Practical and Spiritual Self-Awareness

Faculty of Good Life Sciences.

Part 1

Mandatory Introductory Courses

Course 1

Introduction to the Psychology of the Self-Aware Person

LECTURER: SIGFROID YOUNG
RESEARCHER OF THE HUMAN MIND TODAY

Dear potential student,

In this chapter I address you assuming you are one of the people who understand that the human soul is complex and fascinating and that there is nothing more challenging than it in the world. Throughout generations many researchers of consciousness have tried to map the soul, describe its structure and provide profiles and names to its parts. It turns out there is much more than one possibility available to do so. You have probably already encountered the doctrines of my predecessors and therefore there is no need to repeat them. You can deepen your knowledge from books they have written or on the Internet.

Therefore, in my lecture I shall refer to the structure of the soul, as I understand it. You will find that there is a certain parallel between the structures of the soul in the theories of my predecessors and the structures as I understand them. I have tried to adapt them to the needs of self-awareness. I believe that when we try to map the human soul we have the duty to include the spiritual part.

You see, dear aware one, I believe that the human soul has an eternal element which is the spiritual part of it. So I formulated my own theory which I teach here in this course. Again, I do not pretend to change world psychology. I am just offering you a point of view that will serve you when you strive to develop a strong and confident self-awareness.

So, in my view, the human soul is the personality that a man takes on, being the person he has chosen to be in this lifetime. In addition, the soul also has a higher part, connected directly to the spirit, through which the spirit can communicate with the person.

In my theory, the human soul has four main parts:

1. **The Overt**
2. **The Covert**
3. **The Social**
4. **The Spiritual**

I will clarify each part separately. However, it must be understood that these various parts constantly interact. Also, the relative significance of each part affects the whole personality and is different from person to person. Finally, at

different stages of our lives there will be another part that is more dominant in each of us.

1. The Overt - the conscious mind or the visible personality.

This part usually interests us and is the first one that we try to know and change during the process of self-awareness. At the same time, it is clear to us that its sources are in the other parts and that it is the result of their interaction. Therefore, in order to make the required changes we must examine the rest of the parts. Understanding them will help us find the roots of the visible personality. If a problem lies in one of the other parts, it is up to us to make the changes within them, thereby affecting the **Overt**. It is not always easy and the matter will be discussed in depth during the course itself.

The **Overt** is the part that behaves, thinks and feels, which is perceived by us and by those around us. As already mentioned this is the part we may want to change. Maybe we want to learn to be less touchy or less angry; we want to be more assertive or happier; we seek to foster self-confidence or more generosity or we realize that it will be easier for us to live life if we are less shy or suspicious. These are just a few examples of characteristics, feelings or behaviors that are found in the **Overt**.

2. The Covert - the unconscious part of the mind or the personality that is hidden from the world.

This part is controlled by various fears and it stores a lot of information that can explain our behavior. Memories from different periods including past lives, traumas, suppressed desires, feelings that have not been expressed and skills that have not yet been discovered.

In self-awareness we seek to reveal the **Covert**. Thus there will be less material that directs us out of a secret place in a way we have no control over. We will also be able to express our hidden desires (of course, those that are not destructive) as well as the skills and talents that have been hidden until now.

3. The Social - The part that allows us to adapt ourselves to the society in which we live.

This is part of the soul that is programmed in advance to act based on observations such as "what will they say?" or "that's how it should be". The **Social** is driven by the fear of being rejected or hurt and by the desire to be accepted in society, in our immediate family and by more distant circles. This part causes the **Overt** to act in a manner that will be approved by the community, will be pleasurable and rewarded.

The **Social** part reacts to the environment and shows what it believes others wish to see. Do not misunderstand me, I do not claim that the **Social** part is hypocritical and gives up the truth in order to acquire respect and approval from the environment. Sometimes this is certainly a true description but not always. When the **Social** part works for the benefit of the self and for the good of the environment its actions are effective and positive. There is nothing wrong with the fact that this part seeks recognition or respect and social acceptance. This is natural for us as human beings, and it helps us to be united and maintain a functioning and safe human society for all those who belong to it. I assume that we would like more and more people to develop their **Social** part and to connect to a loving environment and not try to impress, for example, criminal or terrorist organizations which are also a form of social structure.

I realize I may have confused you so I will summarize in saying that the **Social** part's role is to fit us into the society we live in. It contains everything we need to function in our society in the proper and acceptable manner.

4. The Spiritual - this is part of the soul in which the control is transferred to the spirit.

The spirit affects us through intuition, gut feelings and even channeling. This part is the highest and brightest of the structures of the soul. It operates out of infinite and unconditional love. It directs the **Overt** to act independently and honestly.

The **Spiritual** part of the soul has access to transcendent knowledge, both ancient and future, gentle and soft as well as deep and powerful. It may be the most mysterious and beautiful part of the human soul. I believe that not all people have opened, awakened or expressed this part. Unfortunately, not all people recognize the spiritual part of their souls or give it a place in their lives. Those who choose to do so benefit greatly and their lives are more enlightened and lucid than others. I highly recommend you pay attention to the lessons we devote to the **Spiritual**.

There is one more point I wish to bring to your attention regarding the **Spiritual** part of the soul. When someone dies the body and soul also die. The **Spiritual** part however, is eternal. You will learn in a course given by my friend Mr. Joshua of Galilei, "The History of the Self", about previous lives. Therefore, I will only mention the fact that we need to remember that the **Spiritual** part transmits from incarnation to incarnation all that we need to remember. That also includes the lessons and talents we have developed throughout life in a body as well as all the unresolved issues, the lessons that have not been learned and the traumatic experiences that still require healing.

It seems that after describing the four parts of the soul you can understand that there is constant interaction between them and that together they influence the human body. In addition, the entire soul affects the body and is sometimes influenced by it. I am certain that you will learn about this in the "Essentials of the Body-Soul-Spirit" course, presented by another of my colleagues.

Now it is important for me to go over some of the main personality characteristics that I hope to find in self-aware people. You are welcome to examine whether you have them. If you do not, or you have them in the initial phase only, it is strongly recommended that you strengthen them.

What are the qualities that are desirable and useful for self-aware people and that will assist them on their journey?

I would say that primarily **those people must have scholarly curiosity**, especially about the question of the human essence. They should ask themselves questions such as "Who am I?", "What am I?", "What does life mean?" and search for the answers. These people should also be very interested in the way humans act. They should ask questions about their own behavior and the behavior of those around them. The questions will provide them with grounds for countless inquiries. If you tell such a person: "That's the way it is!" he will not settle for that answer. It may surprise you to hear that there are many people who have never wondered who and what they are. If they came across such questions they would seem to them like utter nonsense, a good joke and nothing more. However, self-aware people regard such investigations as the most fascinating and most important thing in the world. Well, maybe not the most important but very important.

After the scholarly curiosity, self-awareness people have an **open mind**! I would ask whether they are able to put aside the familiar and the known, and agree to accept new opinions, alternative explanations and different assumptions. I would most like to know if they have the ability to clear their minds of previous information and come to study with an open mind, free to absorb new knowledge. I am looking for skeptical students who are willing to put a question mark at the end of every sentence. Can you imagine how wonderful it is? After all, if your mind is already full of knowledge, how can you make room for more knowledge? By doubting, examining and filtering every statement and fact repeatedly. Do you agree with me?

Another feature that I think is very necessary for a self-aware person is the **ability to commit**. A person who is willing to go all the way! Someone with patience who does not give up on every obstacle or difficulty. Whether he walks alone or chooses to follow a path where others go, I expect him to start walking determined to move forward despite the ups and downs he will surely meet, despite the obstacles and barriers that will surely emerge, and in any weather!

The next characteristic you should nurture is **the tendency for independence**. You should be independent, with an internal focus control. What does that mean? Someone who does not depend on external factors such as drugs or other stimulants, excitement from entertainment or other peoples' solutions. I want to see students who are resourceful! People who know how to find the answers to problems internally and not via external means! Even when they ask for help, I want to know that they have first tried to help themselves. That the help they receive will be accepted and practiced. Do you understand what I am trying to say? I love people who take action. I love people who believe they are capable! You will find that in various courses you will work on developing and nurturing your own self-belief but I ask you to try very hard to be pre-disposed to independence! Independent thinking, independent behavior, vigorous action. That is what I mean!

There are two other characteristics that I expect to find in my future students. What I am going to say now might sound odd to you but I think you **should be able to rest**. The importance of being able to stop and take time out to relax is tremendous. You have no other way to reboot your internal system, to rewind and to cool your engine. Those who do not know how to rest find themselves quickly burnt out. I hope it does not look so strange to you anymore, my asking for the ability to rest. You will learn to do meditation of various kinds but even going out to work in the garden can reboot your system. Even preparing a salad is sometimes a form of meditation as it clears your head and allows your mind to rest. Do not treat only sleep as rest. Especially since sleep is not always restful. We must know how to rest and relax even when we are awake.

Now I will talk to you about something very interesting. Do you sometimes feel like an alien? Yes, an alien. Are you different, strange and you feel as if you do not belong? Maybe you felt that way as a child and maybe you feel that way occasionally still as an adult? If so, it is great. It tells me you have arrived at just the right place. Moreover, it does not surprise me. **The feeling of separation, of strangeness, of difference** is a feeling that, in my opinion, is a side effect of being a self-investigator. I suppose that self-aware people such as ourselves have a rich inner world from the dawn of their childhood, and are sensitive to themselves and to others. They are also those who always compare themselves to the rest of the world and do not pass through life with ease.

You know what I am talking about. You have often felt unsure, unsuitable. This is something you should be happy about! It means that you are aware of your uniqueness. I hope it did not make you want to be "like everyone else" and try to be who you are not. Because I can tell you, there is no such thing as "everyone else". Each one of us is a unique model, one of a kind! As you progress through self-awareness studies, you will find it is more and more fun for you to be you! You will be happy to discover that you are unique and you will celebrate the uniqueness of your friends and acquaintances. You will learn to cherish and respect the distinctiveness of each person. If you think about it, the more you advance toward the understanding that you are unique and that this is a wonderful thing, we will see that the **Social** part of your soul changes. You will act more out of your inner truth for your own good and for the sake of society and less on "what will they say?" and "what's expected of me?" Don't you think it would be great?

Here I complete my part of this guide. **I have presented to you the structure of the soul and the qualities that characterize the person who chooses self-awareness.** In the next chapter you will familiarize yourself with the course "Essentials of the Body-Soul-Spirit Connection" in which you can understand how the human soul interacts with its body and spirit.

Good luck!

Sincerely,

Sigfroid Young,

Researcher of the Human Mind Today

Course 2

Essentials of the Body-Soul-Spirit Connection

LECTURER: MRS. HOLLY DAY
HOLISTIC STRIVER FOR UNITY

Hello dear and welcome to the introduction to my course.

I have no words to describe to you how important this course is. Well, I have words, of course, do not worry. I urge you to open your ears, open your eyes and especially open your heart wide. Come to this introduction once you are willing to accept everything without judgment and criticism, as a blank page waiting for new information and I promise to provide you with valuable knowledge.

Great. Now that you are free to hear I will tell you about the body, the soul and the spirit. Sometimes people confuse soul and spirit and sometimes they think that the body stands by itself and has no connection to the soul and/or to the spirit, right? Maybe you do not understand what we're talking about either. So I'll try to explain everything in the most direct and simple way. It is important to me that you follow me because if you understand this introduction - I have no doubt that you would very much want to enroll in studies, you would very much want to commit to the way of life of self-awareness from now until the end of time. You will understand how beautiful life is even if it is not always easy or clear to us. Are you ready? Great. We set off.

What is a body? Everyone knows this but I will still give you my definition: this is the physical part that carries us in this life. It consists of dense molecules, just like other physical objects. The body needs proper nourishment, heat and other protective conditions to survive properly. It serves as a sanctuary for the soul including a certain amount of spirit as part of the soul, without which it has no life. The human body is a unique, one-and-only phenomenon and it is an extraordinary machine. For now, this definition will suffice us.

What is a soul? It is the sum total of all thoughts, emotions and the parts of one's personality. The components of the soul are well studied in the psychology course which you read in the previous chapter of my colleague, Mr. Sigfroid Young. He defines the soul as having four parts: the **Overt**, the **Covert**, the **Social** and the **Spiritual**. Remember? So I will allow myself not to dwell here anymore on defining the soul.

The question is what is the spirit? It is a non-physical essence, a divine spark, the immortal essence of man, who he really is since always and forever. It has no limits, it is infinite. Its qualities are unconditional love, infinite generosity, forgiveness, simplicity, wisdom, innocence and lack of judgment. The spirit is the great architect of our lives. Our current lives, those we have already passed and those that we shall pass if necessary. It is the one who plans the personality we will have in every lifetime, where we will be born, to which family and what we will have to learn and do during that lifetime. The spirit has the ability to create, being a divine spark.

Does all this resonate with you as something familiar, my dear? Do you recognize the truth of these things within you? I hope so. I will, however, continue with my explanation.

Well, the spirit sends a part of it to experience a certain reincarnation on earth. For this purpose it wishes to take on a concrete form, to wear a physical body. And this body must be adapted to the program written for the part of the spirit embodied in it, and be equipped with the soul with the appropriate personality. Thus, as the body needs the soul and the spirit to continue to exist - so the spirit needs body and soul to exist on earth.

Let us continue to explore the connections between the three components that form a living being and we will relate, for simplicity, only to a living creature of the human kind. The body lives as long as the energy of life flows through it, or as long as there are spirit and soul.

So life energy passes through the body in one way or another. From the Chinese we learn that it passes through channels called meridians. I have no problem accepting this theory. I presume you do not either. Now, the body should be healthy. In the master plan drawn ages ago, it was designed as a wonderful and precise machine. But we know that in practice, in many cases it is not exactly perfect. Sometimes a baby is born with a disruption - one that is appropriate for the program and for the experiences that he will have to undergo during the course of his life. And also later in life not everything goes well. There are diseases and ailments, injuries and fractures, pains and aches and many other physical problems that we accumulate over time.

Now pay attention. We claim that if there is a problem, it has a reason. And the reason is always in the soul, or to be more precise, in the emotions blocked in it. Emotions that are the result of one's experiences. If during the experience the emotions have an expression - they are not stored inside the person. But if one cannot express the fear, anger, frustration or any other emotion that arises during the event - then they remain and accumulate in the **Overt** and perhaps in the **Covert** part. Are you beginning to get the picture, dear?

After the event itself, as the storm subsides and with the passing of time, it is important to vent the emotions and to release them. You can understand that the difficulty is in reaching the emotions that have been hidden in the **Covert**, right? What's more, if we do not do the work, then the body takes upon itself the expression of the stored material, of the emotions that are asking to be expressed and so it develops a wound, pain or even illness!

The point is, we tend to ignore the distress of the soul and we usually do not stop to see what happened. We tell our self that it must be just fatigue or a passing mood and we try to get over it. We were not taught to find out why we are afraid – just to overcome the fear! And they did not teach us to ask why we are angry, what inner button was pressed inside us – only that it is not nice to be angry! And if we are insulted or envious - we feel ashamed and try to hide it. Right? We do not take the time to stop everything and listen to the emotion, to have a conversation with it, to see why we feel that way.

But when the body develops some symptom - then we pay attention! Then we seek treatment. So the body has no choice but to invent one symptom or another to awaken us from our sleep, shake us and turn on a red light signifying that something is wrong!

Now let's see what medicine does with this red light. Medicine looks at the patient differently when it is Western medicine or alternative medicine. Right?

The approach of modern, Western or conventional medicine is that the symptoms of the body are separate from those of the soul. And the spirit is not taken into account, it is completely out of the picture. Treatment and healing methods include chronic drugs, antibiotics, surgery and in any case treatment is symptomatic. If the illness is in the mental realm, psychiatric drugs are given and they are not always accompanied by conversations. In other words, even in cases of depression or mental dysfunction, they may be satisfied with providing medication without a thorough investigation into the roots of the situation. In conventional medicine it is generally not expected that a person will take responsibility for recovery by changing patterns of thinking and lifestyle - not even by changing his diet, in many cases.

On the other hand, the alternative, integrative or holistic medicine approach, which the self-aware school of medicine also embraces, is that if the body is ill that is a sign that the soul is not completely healthy either. Treat them at the same time! Body-soul medicine.

Also, this approach says that the responsibility for healing is the patient's. The therapist only helps him to help himself. The therapist tries to stimulate the natural healing powers of the body in the least invasive manner possible and he also examines the patient's state of mind. **A body-soul therapist will work with the patient on his self-awareness because that is what will ultimately solve the pain or illness of the body. Together they will work on limiting beliefs, negative thinking patterns, traumas that cause blockage and self-sabotaging habits.**

So much for the body-soul connection.

How does the spirit enter the picture?

I will say it this way - when you remember to relate to the spiritual dimension you can deal with the problem in more depth and reach the reasons behind the reasons and the materials buried very deep in our unconscious, in the **Covert** part of the soul. Sometimes the materials causing the problem are from previous incarnations.

My dear, how are you doing? Can you say that now you understand the body-soul-spirit connection? More or less. I understand. So in my opinion it's time to move on to a subject that will provide us with a gust of fresh air and also demonstrate the body-soul-spirit connection well. Ready?

The Chakras.

Chakras are centers of energy in various parts of the body, which are connected to different organs and physical systems. Through these centers energy is regulated into and out of all organs and systems in the body. When these centers are open to the correct extent our life energy flows properly according to the needs of the different parts of the body: when they need more - it flows in, and when there is an excess that needs release - it flows out. What else? As we said, we have blocks. The emotions that we have not released from past events and which accumulate within us, interfere with the free flow in the meridians and chakras.

When we talk about chakras we usually refer to seven chakras located along the center of the body, the first at the bottom of the pelvis and the seventh on the scalp. **Chakras represent, in addition to physical segments of the body, certain subjects in our mental and spiritual life!**

Can you understand how powerful self-awareness through the chakras is? **Our whole inner world is represented in them!** During your studies with us you will understand this more deeply and you will learn to look at each chakra and diagnose its condition. You will know where there is a weakness that seeks investigation and strengthening, and where there are balance and harmony.

Well, the time has come for us to make an initial acquaintance with the seven main chakras from the bottom up:

Chakra 1.

The Root or Base Chakra. *It is red (and also brown, the color of the earth).*

It is located at the bottom of the pelvis and the base of the spine. It physiologically includes the skeleton, the organs through which waste is removed from the body, the reproductive organs and the gonads. **In the realm of the soul the Root Chakra includes everything related to our sense of existential security: the** feeling that we have solid ground under our feet; that we are protected and are embraced in this world; that we have enough food and money and that we lack nothing. That's if the chakra is balanced, okay? You must be wondering, and rightly so, what happens when it is not balanced. The answer is that then a person has health problems in his organs and systems that are listed and he lives with a sense of existential fear: either he does not feel that the world is safe, or he experiences a fear of abandonment. He is in a state of survival fear. Do you understand? The Base Chakra seeks to give a person a sense of security stemming from connection to the earth, anchoring the roots in solid and fertile soil that can be relied upon! Instead of existential deprivation and fears – it seeks to instill a sense of existential security and abundance.

Chakra 2

The Sacral or Sex Chakra. *It is orange.*

This chakra is in the lower abdomen, below the navel. This region is energetically linked to the hormonal system, digestive juices, kidneys, bladder, genitals and adrenal glands. **In the realm of the soul we are speaking of a person's sexuality and creativity as well as of the vast array of his emotions**. Its energy imbalance will lead to various problems in related systems such as problems with blood flow or impotence. In terms of the soul the imbalance will harm the sensuality and creativity that the person can express. Nor will he express his feelings and desires well. Look at it this way: If life is a stage and the person is an actor - then in an imbalance the actor may be on stage but he does not take his rightful place! He does not bring himself with all his strength and passion! You see? He lives, but not fully. He maintains a life that is not from a place of enthusiasm and desire. And that's too bad. That is why we want to awaken this chakra, to bring it into full and well-balanced action. OK?

Chakra 3

The Solar Plexus Chakra. *It's color is yellow.*

This chakra is located in the area of the diaphragm, rather in the center of the body. It regulates energy for the respiratory system and the diaphragm, the stomach and the digestive system, the adrenal glands, the sympathetic nervous system and the pancreas. **In the realm of the psyche we see the Solar Plexus Chakra as responsible for the self-image of the person and his relationship with society.** That is, how he feels about himself and with those around him. This includes how he perceives and appreciates himself, what kind of relationships he develops with others, and subjects such as self-confidence or courage. When the 3rd chakra is not balanced the person can be isolated, domineering, haunted, anxious or arrogant. On the other hand, tolerance, courage, serenity and sociability - all these attest to the balance of the solar plexus.

Chakra 4

The Heart Chakra. *Its color is green (and pink).*

The heart chakra is the middle of the seven, and is considered to be the one that separates the three lower ones that are connected mainly to the body, and the three upper ones that are more connected to the soul and the spirit. The Heart Chakra is in charge of energy for the following organs: the heart, circulatory system, lungs, immune system, hand-skin and the thymus gland. **On the emotional level we attribute to the Heart Chakra unconditional love, forgiveness, generosity and compassion. Also the ability to give and receive.** Its color is green but also pink. The green is by its place among the seven colors of the rainbow. The pink is the result of mixing red with white. The Heart Chakra, being in the center, is seen as a combination of red and white, the colors of the first and last chakras. Well, dear, what do you think is the role of this chakra in terms of human life? It should contain the ability to give and receive in a balanced manner, the ability to forgive, the ability to see others without criticism and a great degree of mercy. And in general - this is the center of love for myself and for others.

Chakra 5

The Throat Chakra. *It is blue.*

Well, you can guess where that chakra is located ☺ It is responsible for the welfare of the throat and neck, of the vocal cords, thyroid gland, nerves, ears and all the muscles. **As far as the mind is concerned, this chakra refers to our ability to express ourselves, to the extent to which we say what we want to say, ask what we want to ask, verbalize ourselves. It is about communication and inspiration.** Perhaps you notice that there is a connection between the Throat Chakra and the Sacral Chakra. Both are involved in self-expression. Expression of thoughts, desires, opinions and also an expression of talents and skills. When both chakras are balanced the person blooms, he lives fully and creatively and you cannot ignore him! He is full of passion and enthusiasm, glowing in all his colors. It's wonderful!

Chakra 6

The Third Eye Chakra. *It is purple (some say Indigo)*

Here we come to a very special chakra, which is more associated with the level of spirit than the former chakras. The Third Eye Chakra is located at the center of the forehead, between the two eyes and is responsible for the entire head energy - including face, brain, eyes, ears, nose and the pituitary gland. **In the non-physiological field, this chakra is connected to our intuition or to the gut feelings and to telepathy or psychic communication, as well as to the ability to see halos. It is also responsible for balancing both sides of the brain and all their functions - physical and mental.** When the Third Eye Chakra is balanced we make decisions more easily and we are connected to our inner truth, to the source of peace and wisdom within us. If, however, it is unbalanced and perhaps even blocked - there are symptoms of depression, dependency, hearing and vision problems or lack of balance and concentration. Most people are very attracted to the subject of psychic perception and it is really fascinating. But I think the most important role of this energetic center is in the connection of the person to himself!

Chakra 7

The Crown Chakra. *Its color is white (some say purple)*

And now we are in the last, most spiritual chakra of all, the Crown Chakra. It is physically related to the brain. Beyond that, **it is related to the spirit of the person and to the whole universe. Through it we can connect to external energies and to the knowledge that comes from higher realms**. This chakra also excites the human imagination, although I must point out that there are many who reject the possibility of connecting with external and superior worlds. Those people do not know what they're missing! They believe that a person is a closed and separate system that ceases to function completely with death. In the course of life, to their understanding, each of us is to himself, living within his own body. They believe that he is unable to turn outside to receive energies of life and the healing that is right for his body, nor knowledge and answers from nonhuman wisdom. Also, they think that they have no one to direct them from a perspective beyond this life.

Can you see what a loss that is? Too bad. I would like all people to be open, that their Crown Chakra will be balanced. But unfortunately this is not so. At the same time I draw comfort from you, who is reading this guide, and from friends like you. You, who understand how good it is to know that we are not alone! We have someone to lean on, from whom to learn, to seek help, to get advice, to have some loving care! After all, it is so much easier to live with this knowledge! **So the Crown Chakra allows us to connect to high layers of being - to our spirit, to other guides that are souls or beings without body and even to the divine essence**. If the person wants, he can be in a loving relationship with all of these. I highly recommend that! By the way, the Crown Chakra is sometimes associated with the colors of silver and gold.

I can tell you that I myself have seen the colors of chakras on several occasions and they are spectacular. Some people have the ability to see, whenever they want, the chakra colors of those around them and there are those who can photograph the colors and present them through software to all of us. We will teach you to see the state of your chakras through meditation, healing or the use of a pendulum. You will see what color they are, whether they're in a spiral motion, which direction the spiral is spinning at and how fast. From what you see, you will be able to decide whether the chakra is balanced or needs treatment.

If a chakra shows us that there is a problem in its area of control, we will want to bring it back to balance by locating and releasing the blockage when we go deeper into the mental source of it. As you recall, this is the concept of holistic medicine: if the energy blockage is already expressed in the body and there is a medical problem - we are also responsible for the deeper treatment. Sometimes it will lead to healing the physical pain or illness and sometimes we will still also need medical treatment of the body. I am certainly willing to accept a combination of all disciplines for a body-soul-spirit treatment. But **I will never make do with physical therapy alone! I will always want to know what happened in the soul which caused the physical malady, and to deal with the problem at its root**. Does that make sense to you?

I think I can finish my chapter in this manual. We have learned about the mutual connection between the human body and its soul and spirit, with the understanding that they influence one another and do not exist in our lives independently. I have no doubt that I gave you a lot of food for thought, and that while reading the chapter you felt that you were becoming more and more interested in studying self-awareness. You have so much to gain! ☺

You are invited to read the exercises I prepared for you, they are on the next page. You may do them now or come back to them later. Then you can move on to the next chapter, where my friend Mr. Joshua of Galilei will tell you about the source of the human spirit, and what it comes to do when it is incarnated in the body. So exciting!

Goodbye, beloved spirit!

Mrs. Holly Day

Holistic Striver for Unity

Exercises for Chapter 2:

1. **Practice listening to your body** and try to learn how it signals to you about small or large problems. When you are in pain - try to understand what the pain holds, "what's sitting there." Sit in gentle meditation, do not try too hard. Breathe in fully and relax your body muscles. Treat the pain as a friend trying to tell you something. Find ways to help yourself by listening to the subtle signals of the body (butterflies in the stomach, mild pain and muscle tension) as well as the less subtle (disease, intense pain, wounds). This of course does not come in place of medical care, when necessary!

2. **Review each Chakra. Connect with it** in meditation, try to see what color it is and whether it is rotating. Breathe into it the related color. Repeat the exercise occasionally.

3. Read about the Chakras again. **Examine the non-physical context areas of each Chakra in your life**. Ask yourself if there is room for improvement and what can be done to do so. Spend time separately for each Chakra and return to it periodically.

Course 3

On the Source and Purpose of the Spirit

LECTURER: MR. JOSHUA OF GALILEI
A HISTORIAN OF THE VERY DISTANT PAST

Hello dear aware one,

I choose to think of you as an ancient entity, full of deeds and adventures, who wandered over here through the distances of time and space. I wonder if you know you are just that.

Allow me to introduce myself. My name is Joshua of Galilei, and there is a reason. I am connected to Biblical times and to the Old Land of Israel. At least one of my incarnations was then and there. Are you into this matter of past lives and if so - in what way? Because many people are drawn to the subject from a childish fascination, they want to believe that once they were princes or counts or magicians or God knows what. I really prefer you be interested in your previous incarnations from knowing that some of them can help you understand and improve your current life. There is no need to pry into past lives other than for self-awareness purposes. We have enough events to deal with in the current incarnation.

This course is called "On the Source and Purpose of the Spirit". We will learn the history of human spirits. Let us try to understand why this arrangement was created whereby a spirit chooses to let part of it enter a body and come to a life on earth. It's a very fascinating subject, don't you think so?

So let's get started. First of all, I beg you to leave behind all your prejudices, all objections to what you do not know. Open yourself to new information with real readiness. You will be exposed to materials that may be new to you and you may have actually been taught to despise. People tend to mock things that frighten them, it's a way to deal with fear. If I reject something, claiming it is not true or not real - then there is nothing to fear, is there? So there are people who are threatened by ideas such as the eternity of the spirit or a multitude of incarnations. I have no idea why! Anyway, try not to be the kind of person who despises something and denies it without actually knowing enough about it. OK? Do we have a deal? If in the end you decide it is all nonsense, I'll accept your disagreement, and respect your preference.

So at some point in the past the spirits were created. There are those who identify this point in time with the Big Bang. But for us it is like trying to determine when God was created. I prefer to say that spirits are eternal in time. They have always been and will always be. I feel it is also true to say that they are particles of the Divine, they are divine sparks. In this sense, they have the ability to create reality.

Now, you probably ask all kinds of questions like who created the spirits and why he did it. I do not really know, I was not there. But I have all kinds of speculations. God may have created them so that he will not be bored all by himself. Maybe he wished to have someone who sees him, an audience. Because what is the point of being, if no one sees you, right? Perhaps he wanted to develop, and development is made possible by reflecting in others, you will learn about this later in the guide. There is, of course, a possibility that God did not create the spirits but I do not really care. With your permission, I'll say that the souls were created and that's it. OK? Because from this point on I have more confidence in the theory I developed. So go along with my mindset and see what we'll get.

The spirits needed a purpose. Just hovering in the universe is a bit boring and quite pointless, I think. So they decided to come down to the world, to arrange a kind of lively amusement park where they could experience and have fun. And so they began to reincarnate. That is - to come again and again to life on earth. Just like children climb again and again onto a slide. It is possible that the spirits did not immediately get human bodies, I'm not sure about that. But once they started doing it, they fell in love with it and have been going on and on ever since. So you are a spirit in one life out of many you had, and perhaps will still have. There is, of course, also the possibility that you are a spirit having your first incarnation on earth. What do you think of these ideas dear? Do you like them?

If the idea of incarnations is not agreeable to you, maybe it's because life does not look like such a big thing. And so you do not understand how you can fall in love with them and want to come back again and again! In that case, I can understand you but look at it this way: the spirit is fundamentally made of energy, an intelligent and loving energy, just as I want to imagine God. Infinite energy, all wisdom and unconditional love. When the spirit comes into this world it does not come like that. It must shrink itself, compress a part of it so that it can fit in a physical body. If all the spirits embodied in a human form were pure love - what exactly would they have to do here? Again they would fall into hopeless boredom! No, no, it would not work. They had to invent something that would bring interest and meaning into the picture.

So to prevent boredom every soul that descends into a human body takes on her journey a bag full of trouble, drawbacks and lessons to learn. It is impossible to be born into a new life without shouldering a bag like this, although its size and weight may vary. To add interest and experience to life, so that it would have more depth, it was necessary to create things that would serve the senses. If people can feel, stroke or be injured; If people can taste and decide what tastes good and what does not, what makes them feel good in the stomach and what harms them; If there is beauty and ugliness in the world, lovely sights and terrifying sights; Or if you can hear sounds and noises of different kinds - then life is really a spectacular amusement park.

So what am I saying? I urge you not to think about life as difficult or about the universe as threatening. Life is for you! You can see in any difficulty or obstacle a simple facility in the large amusement park that your spirit chose to visit. It has probably been here many times, your wonderful spirit, you just do not remember. You cannot remember, that's part of the game. When the spirit-part loads the bag onto its back and enters a new body, it agrees to forget everything it has learned until then. Because otherwise it's no challenge, it's no fun.

So when the person is born he does not remember who he is and what he already knows. Every so often he opens his bag of surprises and pokes. He is exposed to another detail of the journey that his spirit had planned for him. At first he knows himself as he sees himself in his parents' eyes. Hopefully they admire him and think he is the best thing that happened to them. There comes a stage when he meets his main weakness - the one that will cause him the most pain but will also push him forward. At another stage he discovers he has a special talent, maybe he manages to play music or win the school running contest. At some point it turns out that someone loves him very much or maybe not. Along the way he learns what he can achieve in the world, how he can affect others and what he loves or hates. You have to admit it's very, very interesting! Life is a totally unexpected adventure and that's the beauty of it! But just as we are filled with wonder and gratitude, we are also filled with fear.

Now, how does self-awareness fit into this whole beautiful story? It goes like this: Some people start at a certain point of life to remember. That is - they are becoming aware. It can start very dimly and then they ask themselves "Who am I?", "What am I?", "What does life mean?" They wonder whether there is a superior purpose to their being born, to the fact that there is a world inhabited by people who live in a variety of conditions and situations, sometimes with joy and sometimes with sorrow. Later they wonder if they have a role to play, a mission.

Maybe you remember when you started to wake up. Did you ask these questions? Perhaps you did not know you were asking, a subconscious part of you asked for you. In that case, maybe one day something happened to you that made you remember. Some people see a vision, others all at once perceive their unity with all creation or they have an outer body experience. **Some people remember slowly, others are reminded with a BOOM, and some are not reminded until the day they die**. The last option is really unfortunate, because these people are missing a great part of the fun. Most of those who continue to sleep cannot ever see the light, but remain in the frightening darkness of the world, on the shadowy side of life. Unfortunately we hear about this side endlessly in the news and there is a sense that quite a few people get stuck there and do not develop, do not wake up, do not remember that they are actually spirits who are beings of love.

I have to point out that there are also good people who navigate through life easily and choose the light, but they do not deal with complex questions such as "Who am I and what is my purpose?" They just live. Know such people? They probably came with a not very heavy bag, and they do not need to wrack their brains. Or break their heart. That's all according to the plan of the spirit. On the other hand, sometimes people who did come with a full bag, go through life not agreeing to open their eyes and learn their lessons and then life gives them a blow. I hope it works, that at least then they wake up and understand what they've come to do here. Why is this important? Because at first those are small blows, but as the people do not wake up, the blows become stronger. What's more, what we have not done here in this lifetime will pass on, to some life in the future.

And here I want to talk to you about the subject called "**Karma**". **When the past affects the present and even the future**. Karma is like a bank account that we have at a virtual branch somewhere in infinity. When we do a good deed, we get credit points and when we have to be punished, we lose points. No, no!!! I'm just kidding with you. It's not like that. **Karma talks about deeds and consequences. There is a match between them.** What are you saying there? That it sound the same to you? You're not alone in that feeling but it's really not the same. Deeds and consequences are not like reward and punishment. I do not think that anyone rewards us for good or correct deeds and punishes us for bad deeds or for mistakes we make! The results tell us whether we acted correctly, whether we did something that promotes us or not. And so, through trial and error, we can improve and fine-tune our conduct. It's very simple.

I want to summarize: In every human there is a spiritual part that is a divine spark, which decided to come to experience this life according to a list of specific experiences and tasks set before this person was born. By the way, his parents and all his living conditions were also chosen for him in advance so that they would serve the goals of his specific program. Some say that the day of birth and the day of death are also determined in advance and that this means that they are not determined by chance. I do not know about it, but I'm willing to agree. What about you? Can you remain open minded to the whole theory I'm laying before you? Excellent! Well done. I really appreciate it ☺

To finish our summary, the person experiences life through the stages of his spirits' plan, and he is supposed to remember slowly who he really is: with a spirit that is like God, good and wise, loving unconditionally, eternal and capable of creation. He also fills his part of the contract and does his homework: repairing old damages, improving himself, making peace in places he once fought and hurt ... Do you understand? The awake and aware human being tries to understand the signals and cues he receives throughout life in order to live according to the plan he intended for himself even before he was born, in the interval between the previous incarnation and the present one.

My dear, I think for now that is all on my part. I gave you the main points of the introduction to my course. In the course itself I teach how we can read the signals and decipher the clues. Since I teach the history of the distant past, i.e. past incarnations, you can guess that I teach how to find out which of those incarnations cause problems and difficulties in the current incarnation. It helps to understand what is happening to you in this life and why. I also teach to close unfinished business from there, to deal with the pains that come from that time, and to make better choices than those made in that distant past.

So what are you saying? Did I convince you? Can you accept my explanations and the existence of past lifetimes? It seems to me that the thought that we have an eternal part that has seen almost everything and will exist even after this life is over, can be very comforting.

Thank you for reading this article of mine, all the best and good luck with reading the rest of this guide. In the next chapter you will learn about an important and central subject in self-awareness: the inner child!

See you in class!

Yours truly,

Joshua of Galilei,

A Historian of the Very Distant Past

Part 2

Getting to Know Yourself

Course 4

Childhood and the Inner Child

LECTURER: MS. JOY LITTLE
AN EXPERT ON THE INFLUENCE OF MEMORIES

D ear child,

I see that you accompanied today your late manifestation, the almost-mature man you became, and you tagged along to see if he would decide to enroll in our curriculum. In case he registers - we will be very happy to host you too. Yes, I know you go with him everywhere. I know, but **he** doesn't, right? And we may have frightened him a little now, so with your permission I'll address him too. OK sweetheart?

So - dear potential student!

I am happy to present you with the main points of my course, in order to make it easier for you to decide whether to register or not. You probably read the paragraph above, so you already know that I, as a lecturer and as a most aware person, turn first to your inner child, the child you once were and that still exists within you. You go everywhere together! You may find this odd, and it is not always pleasant to think that it is so ... um ... yes ... I can imagine. But that's how it is.

Sometimes our inner child is actually quite mature and independent. This is in the better cases, in which we had a warm and supportive home and we did not encounter too many situations in which we were hurt, diminished, insulted, frightened or abandoned. You know, situations that the child does not have the means to deal with. But it is very rare to find someone who has never encountered such unfortunate situations. Most people have a load of memories and childhood experiences that were not pleasant to their inner child back then, in childhood itself, and are no more pleasant to him today. Maybe it's even a very heavy load.

So your inner child, my friend, dwells inside you. You carry him everywhere. And assuming you are a normal person who falls within the normal range, you and your inner child have many unresolved matters, difficult feelings and a lot of pain. You share this burden but he is more aware of it. You can say that he carries the burden for you and allows you to ignore both: the burden and the child. This arrangement is very convenient for you, but it's not healthy, it's not good. Not for the child, and not for you. And in my course you will have to acknowledge his existence, meet him, hear his stories and feel his pain. Moreover, you will find yourself connecting to him, your heart will go out to him and it may not be easy. Next you will be required to help him process the experiences and release the painful and frightening baggage that he could not forget. **It is only through the processing of the traumatic memories of the child that you or will be able to dismantle the load, forgive, forget, heal and then grow up.**

In case I did not explain myself properly, and you still do not understand what I'm talking about, I'll try to explain the issue of the inner child in other words. OK? We are today very much a product of who we were as children, and then we were a product of the baggage we were born with – that of our genetic code and from previous incarnations - together with the experiences, since birth, at home and outside. If there are traits that we want to change in ourselves today, we should take care of them in the level of the inner child. There we may be able to see the source of those traits and take care of them, or at least we can give our inner child confidence and love so that he can overcome any difficulty himself. That is, we have the option of doing in depth treatment!

From your visits to the dentist you know that root canal treatment is not the easiest treatment - but not the worst. There is life after it and it is a better life. **Root canal treatment is what this course offers you. You will learn how to contact your inner child, you will connect with him emotionally, hear from him what is heavy on him and you can give him your wisdom and experience, as well as warmth and love**. You have no idea what a change this will make in your life! You'll just grow up and your behavior will be more confident and mature. You'll be at peace with yourself and with the world.

You see, the little kid needs you. But you need him, too. Together, you must shed light on the events from the conscious memory, the **Overt** part, or from the unconscious, the **Covert** part of the soul, and then unburden the sadness, insult or anger from your childhood. After this process of cleaning it is very important to try to forgive and, if possible, forget.

We use different techniques for this purpose - mainly in writing and in guided imagery. In the exercises at the end of the chapter you will find three exercises that can give you a taste of these techniques. You should do them, believe me.

I want to tell you something else. After you do the work and take the load off the small shoulders **do not be in a hurry to cut yourself off from the child you were.** We strive to teach you how to help him become healthier, more confident and happy - and then stay with you and accompany you positively! He will no longer make you feel small and confused, worthless and weak, angry and offended, as before. Now he will bring to your life the quality of a happy child! You'll find yourself dancing just like that, jumping in puddles after the rain, smiling at people you do not know and going back to playing.

You see, **it is good for us to never stop being a bit like children.** When was the last time you went wild? When did you run and jump and laugh with all your heart? When did you lie on your back and watch the clouds sail in the sky? It's a lot of fun. They make all kinds of shapes, and whoever guesses them right gets a kiss on the heart. Yes, yes! Try it!

What I'm trying to tell you is that life is worth living as if it was a playground. And to this playground you have to come somewhat naively, with the ability to trust and surrender. Who can live like this? Only small children. And you have a built-in child! He is already a structured part that you have lived with all these years, without paying attention to him. So do start, start to see him and strengthen him; be some kind of older brother to him and let both of you learn from each other. This way you can live a life of responsibility and of promoting action, but also remember to rejoice, to have fun, to play the game of life.

Wise and beloved awareness-seeker - both the child and the adult who are you - I will finish my part of this guide. I urge you not to hesitate too much. Registration to our department is always open but it's a pity, every moment that you're not in class! The last classes yielded masses of more enlightened, happier people, in whose lives there had been developments that were not even an imaginable possibility for them before!

The next course deals with self-esteem and self-acceptance, which are a direct and important continuation of self-awareness work. You'll enjoy it!

Have a happy day,

Give a huge hug to the child within you,

Love,

Ms. Joy Little.

Exercises for Chapter 4:

1. **Meditation of the home in which you grew up**: enter a relaxed state. When you are calm and breathing slowly, see yourself reaching your childhood home. See who is there, meet your parents and see yourself as a child. Play with the child that is you, talk to him, and hug him. Take the time to tour the rooms. Open doors, closets and drawers. When you are finished, slowly come out of the meditation, and write down the emotions that came up and what you saw. You may want to repeat this meditation several times. If feelings arise - let them be, they will clean out and pass. If this exercise is too difficult for you emotionally, do not do it alone.

2. **Write a letter to your inner child**. Tell her what you know she is experiencing. Share with her what you feel about her, and update her with changes that have occurred in you from her age to the present.

3. **You can write yourself a letter from your inner child**. Let him express himself. Write fluently, without thinking. It is not a matter of inventing a letter, but of providing a platform for the child to express himself. Whatever is on his heart - is still on your heart! Let it all out on paper.

Course 5

Self-Esteem and Self-Acceptance

LECTURER: MR. A. SMART
AN EXPERT IN KNOWING YOURSELF

Young man, greetings.

I appreciate your being here. It is not obvious. The truth is, nothing should be obvious. Did you get up this morning and the sun was shining? Say thank you! Be happy and excited about it! It is not obvious! Lol, man, appreciate it!

And that brings me straight to the heart of our business. Appreciation. Especially self-appreciation or self-esteem. Boy Oh Boy. Self-Esteem. What a complicated subject. I cannot exaggerate its importance and its complexity. If there is only one course you will learn from our self-awareness program - it must be this course. And not because I'm giving it. No, no. Because it is a subject that is in your highest interest. Again - I do not exaggerate. If there is one thing without which life cannot be good - it is high self-esteem. At least self-esteem which aspires to be high. High self-esteem is the basis for self-acceptance. So think about them together – self-esteem and self-acceptance. Because how can you accept yourself if you do not think you're worth it? If you do not appreciate yourself? It's impossible. Trust me.

I'll ask you something else. How can you evaluate yourself if you do not know who you are? If you do not know yourself? That too is not really possible. It does not make sense. So we shall work this way in the course itself: **we will start with self-acquaintance, then we will turn to self-esteem and finally we will get to self-acceptance**. Is that okay with you? I hope so. And if now in our conversation sometimes I will mix the three areas a bit, do not be angry with me, it does not really matter. Because in life there really is not a clear separation between them, right? The important thing is that **in the end you will learn to accept yourself and be at peace with the fact that you are who you are**. Why is this important? Because then you will be able to respect and love yourself. Wow. Can you imagine how it will feel? Take a moment to close your eyes and try to sense it: appreciation ... acceptance ... respect ... love ... for yourself. For the person who is you...

How lovely. It is so exciting! Isn't it?

Listen, buddy, I hope I've been able to get you to understand how important it is to cultivate self-esteem and self-acceptance. Now you must be muttering to yourself: "Come on, man, but how do you do that?" So I ask you not to hurry. I'll answer you but it will take some time. I'll just let the words speak for themselves, and please let yourself listen and get carried away with the words. Here I go.

When you were born, a huge spirit in a tiny body, you were a puzzle to your parents. They expected a lot from you but they really did not know what to anticipate. Neither did you. Just like them, you did not know who you were or what kind of person you were going to be. You only knew, in the most instinctive way, that these beings who play the role of your parents should give you everything you need to survive and grow. And you had a loud voice that demanded it from them. You thought to yourself in your little heart or maybe in your little head, that you deserve it! You deserve food, and clothes, and protection and a hug. You deserve to be accepted and loved unconditionally. You were not aware that you bothered them sometimes and exhausted them with your screams, or that you are causing them frustration because they do not always manage to figure out what the hell you want! You were small and charming and trusted those who took care of you. You were confident that they knew what they were doing. Mostly you believed they wanted the best for you.

As time went on and you grew up, small cracks began to form in the protecting shell you felt you were born with. When did they start to form? It depends on how things went according to your own plan. Yes? I dare say that the cracks in your trust and sense of protection have already begun in the delivery room. Think about it - birth in the modern era is a really cruel process. The newborn comes out of the silence and darkness of the womb quite violently. He is pushed out by force! And if that were not enough, at the end of the bullying and pressing birth canal he is shot out into a strong light! Into cold air! Into loud noise! All his senses are bombarded at once without any softening! Without any understanding or consideration! Can you feel it? Horror. I just do not understand how we continue to give birth like that for so many years! And all over the world! How is that still so? Wait a minute, let me relax. Deep breath...

I consider it a crime. And it does not end there. Right? Because now they are quick to cut the umbilical cord which is still thumping and still has a role. And then instead of wrapping the baby and letting his mother hold him to her, so as to warm and cradle and calm him - what do we do? Slap him hard so he will start to scream his lungs out and take him to weigh. Tell me, why is it more important to weigh him right now, on the hard and cold scale? Why? I tell you, it makes me so angry. I hear about mothers asking for the baby and at the hospital they tell them to rest, to let the staff do the baby's tests without them, without the father, and forsake the soft little creature in a room full of babies with not enough responsible adults available to take care of them. Yes, I said they forsake him. Have you ever seen what this room looks like? Babies cry until they choke, crushed to the side of the cradle and smeared with their emissions. The heart aches from only thinking about it. But let's move on. It is fortunate that there are already places that offer a more natural and humane birth process.

Now the cute little one is brought home. Here it's warm and pleasant, he's protected and cared for and everything's fine. In most cases it really is so. And the days go by. The baby gets acquainted with himself. At first he does not separate himself from the world, everything is mixed up, and slowly he develops a perception that he is separate from Mom, from Dad, from his bed, and so on. There is himself - and there is everything else. And as stated, according to his understanding, everything else is meant to serve him. Over time, the cracks I mentioned are widened and he learns that his crying does not always fetch Mom, she does not always do what pleases him and in general he is not always understood. Even when he is already beginning to express himself not only with shrieks. He points, he smiles, he shakes his head as a sign of yes and no, he even speaks. Yet his control over things is not perfect. Slowly he begins to formulate a perception of what he is worth, what his value is.

It goes something like this: "If Mom laughs at me and feeds me patiently - I'm good, I'm loved. But if she's angry and her gestures are nervous - I've done something wrong, I'm bad, maybe she does not love me anymore. If Mom and Dad are arguing - it's probably because of me, it's my fault". We can imagine the emotional roller-coaster experienced by a small child on a daily basis, and it is not simple. Can you see that? When he feels accepted and appreciated by the adults around him - his value rises in his own eyes. If, on the other hand, they are not focused on is needs or are in any way displeased with him - his self-worth declines.

When he grows up people from outside the family enter the picture - caregivers, teachers, other children, the parents of the other children and people at the grocery store. The whole world joins the judicial panel that tells the child when he is okay and when not; when he is worth a lot and when less; whether he is highly valued or is not good enough. God, how can you live like this? I truly believe that it is very difficult to be a child.

If you think about it, our self-worth rises and falls all through childhood and adolescence. I do not know if anyone has developed self-esteem before finishing adolescence, that is, before he became a young person. Only then, perhaps! Only then would he be able to stop changing his opinion of himself according to each glance that the girl he loved gave or did not give in his direction;

according to each teacher's attitude toward him; according to his social status in the various classes or his relationship with his parents and siblings. It's crazy!

And if after all this you have come out sane, healthy, even upright and quite self-sufficient - it's a miracle. I'm going back to the beginning of my conversation with you - that's not self-evident! So I, when I meet you, I appreciate you. In advance. Without knowing you. And I appreciate every one of the people who survived and have reached this point. You are walking miracles! Well done!

I have described some difficult experiences and perhaps scared you. You ask yourself what do I want and why do you need to hear me. So listen, if you had an idyllic picture of your childhood – I do not wish to smash it. You can decide to keep it intact. Frame it and hang in the living room, I have no problem with that. My friend from the course on the inner child will already do what needs to be done with it. **As for me, I will take you in my course through a thorough investigation of your present personality in your own eyes. I assure you that it will be fascinating, surprising, exhilarating and, above all, a basis for strengthening your self-esteem.**

When you join my classroom, **you will be given tools to look at yourself.** You will be able to find out what you think about yourself deep inside, even in the **Covert**, the unconscious part of your soul. You will get deeply acquainted with yourself as you've never done before. You will learn what your weaknesses are and what your strong points are; what you unconsciously say to yourself and how it affects your feeling and behavior; what beliefs you have below the surface that dictate your choices; what you are afraid of, what you are angry about, what ancient insults you still carry - everything that is in the mysteries of your being and affects so much who you are and what your life looks like. What do you say, is this a good deal? You're not sure. So let me tell you what you'll get out of it, what good will it do you to delve into your less familiar part. Are you ready?

After you know yourself all over and deep down, you can formulate your self-perception again. You can decide whether you are worthy of your own respect and of that of others, but now you can do it on the basis of the truth. You will know who you are and whether you can be trusted and first of all whether you can believe in yourself and in your abilities.

You can, if you wish, strive to change what you do not like. If you find that you have **thoughts** that do not serve you well - you can replace them with thoughts that will advance you! If you find that you have **feelings** that are old and stale or that they are burdensome to you without any positive value, you can do a job of deconstructing these feelings and replacing them with emotions of high energy frequency such as joy and forgiveness! And you can also change **behaviors** that are not pleasant to you and that do not open up a positive and constructive chain of responses.

You may wonder what you will do if you find that you have patterns of thinking or behavior that you cannot change! Maybe you've already tried, and it has not happened, you're just like that and that's it. For instance - maybe you wanted to be more sociable, but you hold out only a short time before your heart calls you back to your warm, comfortable solitude. Or you may have hoped to become an animal-loving person because it seems to you that animal lovers are more humane - but as much as you try you cannot really relate to animals. So what should you do? You can keep trying, maybe perseverance will pay off and you will succeed - or you can give up and say to yourself: **"That's me,**

and I'm okay!" You agree to recognize a trait or behavior as part of who you are - and to **accept yourself just like that. There are times when you have to agree to be as you are, unchanged.** I'm like that, and it's okay.

What do you mean I'm like that and it's okay? And if it is not okay? So let me say here that of course I refer to behaviors that do not harm others or yourself.

It is also very important for me to say that everyone is worthy. Tell yourself: **"I am inherently good and worthy of appreciation!"** And listen to me, if you decide you can appreciate yourself, respect the person you are, accept what cannot be changed and even what can be changed but you have not changed yet - you'll see that everything becomes much easier for you. You know why? Because you are your own worst critic. When you begin to show more forgiveness and acceptance toward yourself, when you agree to see everything that is beautiful and good in you - and add to it the idea that no one is perfect - life will seem easier to you, the sky more blue, the air sweeter, and the fields abloom. Man! That would be great! You yourself will release you from the chains of self-criticism and go free. Do you understand?

I talk to you about self-esteem and self-acceptance in all areas of your life: regarding your body, your character, your patterns of thinking, your profession and your social status, your achievements and failures - every aspect of who you are today. **You will reach a state of being reconciled with yourself, and of agreeing to be you.** This will have a side effect that will probably make you happy - **the people around you will also begin to appreciate and accept you more!** You will project the quality of a person who is more self-assured, more upright, and anyone who sees you will not be able to ignore it. People tend to automatically adopt a person's view of himself.

Do you remember me telling you at the beginning of our conversation that in my scholarly opinion there is no more important course than this one? I hope you remember and more importantly I hope that now you also agree with me. So I want to invite you to start cultivating self-esteem and self-acceptance right now.

At the end of this chapter I wrote some exercises for you on the subjects of my course. Exercises that will help you make friends with your body, get to know the features you like and dislike in yourself, and locate patterns of thinking that manage you and that may need changing. These exercises will give you a taste of what we do together in class. Please take the time to do them, the exercises, because I am in favor of you earning something by buying and reading this guide before you even register at our department. I think that investing in yourself will in itself be a step of self-esteem. What do you say, we have a deal? Terrific.

I must part with you here and clear the stage for my friend, Miss Heart, and her course: "The Importance of Self-Love." Be good to yourself and remember that I am all sincere admiration for you already!

With infinite respect and appreciation,

Mr. A. Smart,

An Expert in Knowing Yourself.

Exercises for Chapter 5:

1. **Start making friends with your body**. Here are some ways to do so:

   A. Sit in front of a mirror and look at your face. Take the time to study your expressions. Look into your eyes. Tell yourself strong words of acceptance and appreciation.

   B. When you are alone, stand in front of a full-length mirror without clothes. Look at your body. It's not an easy exercise, most people are very critical of their bodies. Repeat this exercise often until you get used to seeing your naked body. It is very important to know the body and accept it, even if you try to make changes. Remember that a weight loss diet or a muscle strengthening plan will achieve their goal much better when you accept and love yourself than when you are full of guilt, self-disgust, anger or shame. It's your body, you need it, and it needs to be accepted and nurtured by you.

2. **Get to know the features you like and do not like in yourself**. Make two lists labeled "like" and "dislike" and fill them persistently, over a period of time. Whenever you recall another feature add it to the appropriate list. Finally, look at the notes again. Make decisions to change what you want and can, and follow through. Make peace with whatever you want

to change but you cannot. Be happy with your good qualities and cultivate them!

3. Try to **pay attention to repetitive patterns of thinking** that do not advance you. Especially those of self-criticism, lack of trust in your abilities, and other belittling and limiting thoughts. Repeat the mantra: "I am inherently good and worthy, just as I am" or any similar mantra that resonates with you, and supports self-acceptance.

4. Hang up the following sentences in a noticeable place and read them often:

> *I am willing to be aware of all my aspects -*
>
> *the better and the worse,*
>
> *the ones that serve me and those that block me.*
>
> *I am willing to be me wholly -*
>
> *with all my facets and aspects that I know!*
>
> *I am willing to acknowledge the facts about myself and not to deny them, willing to live by them and feel good about it!*

Course 6

The Importance of Self-Love

LECTURER: MISS HEART

FOUNDER OF "I LOVE ME"

O h, there you are. Wonderful. I'm so glad you came!

Sit down comfortably and we'll start right away. Are you sitting? Comfy? Great.

Well, if you have read the previous introduction you probably remember that it says that self-esteem and self-acceptance lead to the possibility of nurturing self-love. And they do. I would say that self-love is very important because we all need love. Love is the force of life, it is a wonderful energy. Everything is made of love, **love is the basic energy of all that exists**. God is pure love and great figures from the past embodied such love. This attracted fans and worshipers, a large crowd of supporters who followed them. I will not give you an example here, so as not to provoke competition between religions. But remind me when we meet in class and I'll tell you. You know what? It is very likely that figures of love are walking among us today. It is so much fun to think like that! Dense love in the form of a human being.

I said that everyone needs love. It is an existential need of ours, like breathable air. There is evidence that babies who do not receive love are emotionally and mentally hurt. They may even die. You are welcome to search it online. We need love not only as infants but throughout life. Love is a nourishing and supportive force, it is the essence of life and the most important medicine. Yes, yes, that's right, love is healing. I suppose you agree with me that we all very much want it, even if we can manage without it. Right? Who doesn't want love?

The point is, there are not always people around us who love us. We may live on our own or work in an indifferent place or belong to a family where love is not expressed. So what do we do? We love ourselves! **Each of us should know how to give love to himself.** That's why we have a course called "The Importance of Self-Love."

I hope it is clear that we are not talking about the situation in which a person is too much in love with himself, selfishly or blindly and certainly not in a narcissistic way. It's much simpler than that - **you love yourself unrelated to other people.** There is no importance to questions like whether they love you back, or whether you love yourself more than you love them. When you have true love, it is enough for yourself and also to give it to others. You'll never run out of love, assuming it is true love.

What is true love? Such that does not depend on anything! That is, you can love someone regardless of his or her achievements, and regardless of whether they love you back. You love and that's all. Simple! And in the same way you can love yourself too.

Well, it really sounds simple, but somehow people manage to complicate it. It is very rare to meet a love that is free from any context, free from any conditioning. Right? And this is an excellent reason to develop self-love. That way at least one person will love us unconditionally, no matter what we do: whether we succeed or fail, whether we look good or not and even if we sometimes are not very nice. **Self-love should be available to us always and unconditionally.**

Another point to establish the importance of love for oneself is that when you radiate out love - it is reflected back to you. People who meet you see a lovable person! I will add the sentence "like attracts like" that you probably already heard. It belongs here. **Send out love - and you'll also attract love.** It's much more worthwhile and pleasant than attracting criticism, jealousy, malice or other feelings of this kind – isn't it?

Now I have a very important question for you: Do you love yourself?

I believe the answer popped in your head as soon as you read the question, you did not have to think too much. If you answered "yes" - you belong to a lucky minority because most people cannot honestly say that they love themselves. The more common answer is "no" or maybe something more subtle like "not so much", "sometimes yes and sometimes not" and answers like that. Does that surprise you?

A person's ability to love himself is developed from early childhood, and is based on his self-esteem and self-acceptance. And since it is not so obvious that he will develop them to a high level, as my colleague told you in the previous course, it is no wonder that the result is that most people, before they embrace the self-awareness way of life, do not really like themselves. Instead they criticize themselves, are angry with themselves or ashamed of themselves – which of course is pretty bad. I suppose you know what I'm talking about, you recognize these patterns of thinking and feeling from yourself or your friends. The fact is that most children grow up to be adults who are not pleased with themselves. There are quite a few things they would like to change.

How does self-love manifest itself in our daily lives? Beyond feeling good about myself and not criticizing myself or being embarrassed by who I am, **how will I manage my life when I love myself?** Let me proceed to give you some expressions of healthy self-love.

When you love yourself you will be attentive to your needs and desires. You will listen to your body - you will notice its signs of distress even when they are primary, pay attention to any discomfort and know how to ask the body what is happening and what it needs you to do. This will make you, for example, pour yourself a large glass of water instead of taking something to eat because you will understand that you are actually thirsty. And maybe you'll realize you're not breathing freely and fully, and you will pause to take a few deep breaths. Or you'll notice how much your shoulders need rest and you'll relax them and feel relief. Do you understand, my dear? Your self-love will include your body. You will not forget to take care of it and look after it, **you'll be in a loving relationship with your body**. And in response you will have a wonderful shield to walk in through life. The body will support you, contain you, function well for you and it will do something else for you: it will continue to signal when something is not quite right, it will turn on red lights to attract your attention. At first the signals will be very subtle - and only if you do not pay attention will your body increase them. Over time you will learn to recognize them when they are mild and respond to them. That will be very pleasant! You will know how to help yourself and how to give your body the best conditions for it to be strong and healthy.

The signals that your body will send - and of course it is sending to you even now - will tell you not only about physical distress. Very often they will testify to an emotional storm beneath the surface, repressed heartache, an untreated emotion or information from the **Covert** part of the soul, all of which require your attention. You can say that the body serves as a mediator between the subconscious part of the soul - the **Covert** and the conscious part - the **Overt**. When you love yourself, you will know how to identify the distress of the soul directly and so less and less will the body need to signal you. Then it will be freer to maintain itself, digest food, remove waste and deal with hazards. In short - **when you love yourself you will be more physically and mentally healthy.**

In addition, **self-love will let you treat yourself with respect**. You will not agree to be in places and situations that you do not like, that you're not happy with. You will not hold on to a job that does not fulfill and reward you well and you will not stay in touch with people who either deprive you of energy or belittle you. You will look for ways to have fun, grow, develop and express yourself.

Self-love makes sure that we know the things that make us happy and we bring more of them into our lives. It makes sure that we are involved in activities that charge us with energy and activities that bring us together with people with whom we have good chemistry. With self-love we make a point of choosing how to split our time between tasks and duties, entertainment and pleasure. This balance is very important.

Can you think of the things you do for yourself out of love? I added exercises for you right after the chapter. Take time to do them, this effort will in itself be an act of self-love. Because **those who love themselves stop occasionally to ask: "How am I?"** They pause to examine their situation, to check different areas of their life. So I've given you exercises to help you understand whether you love yourself in the deepest and best possible way. You can draw yourself a clear picture of your self-love. Is it not worthwhile?

At this point you are invited, if you wish, to stop reading and go to practice. Sit quietly with writing tools and let the exercises take you on an inner tour of your love to the person who is you.

There is another level of self-love that we have not mentioned - the level of the spirit. What will happen to your relationship with your spirit when you love yourself? Your spirit will begin to be revealed to you more clearly! You will find that you are increasingly asking to consult with it, to receive treatment from it and to talk to it. Your spirit will help you to love yourself more deeply. The connection with your spirit will allow you the profound inquiry that was mentioned to you before - including the study of previous incarnations - and you can do the necessary cleaning and healing work of self-awareness from a non-judgmental place, without self-blame, and with respect and compassion for who you were in the past and who you are today. The spirit holds for you a tremendous treasure of knowledge and wisdom, it can direct you to extraordinary achievements and to increased effective and useful self-expression.

Listen to me child, **life with a connection to your spirit is like life from another league!** Because the spirit is your essence, and living when you are attached to this essence means that you can live on a daily basis out of love for yourself and for the whole world. This is because your spirit is very clean, generous, forgiving and soft. It has time, it is in no hurry and not stressed out. **Life according to the spirit is quieter and more comfortable because there is no need to compete - there is enough of everything for everyone. Looking at the world from the eyes of the spirit is a loving and compassionate way of looking, from a point of view that knows that you have a safe place and that you have presence even if you do nothing.** You will find that you can enter a room full of people you have never met before - and feel comfortable. You will sit down in one of the seats and be quiet and calm, look around with an open gaze and your peace will bring the others to you. They will recognize that you love yourself and are comfortable in your skin. Some will approach you because you will reflect back to them what they would also like to have. Others will be attracted to you because they too are people who love themselves - they will recognize you as someone who resembles them.

When you live your daily life from the place of the loving spirit you discover, for example, that when you drive on the road calmly, when you are kind and courteous to the other drivers, when you look forward to a safe and pleasant driving then suddenly all the other drivers will be polite, they will not rush anywhere and the road will look like a calm river to you. You will flow smoothly and sing with the radio from a happy heart. Yes, yes, that's what will happen! Even if you usually think the road is a madhouse or a battlefield. I tell you - when you set out to drive with a full expectation of enjoyable driving - that's what you'll meet in reality. How can it be? Because when you request good things and align yourself with them, when you yourself choose to live on the level of the spirit - then your spirit can create a reality for you accordingly! Your spirit is a divine spark, remember? And the divine knows how to create.

Now look. Why is this course essential? After all, you can wake up in the morning and say to yourself: "Today I will have a wonderful day, I'll love the whole world and the world will love me back!" Well, if you wake up like that every morning that's wonderful! If those words you say come from the depths of your heart and will be backed by an inner feeling of joy and thanksgiving - then really, what can I tell you? You can be released from this course. Perhaps you can yourself write a self-awareness guide or teach a course.

But … how can I say it … I doubt that this is the case. And I'll tell you why. I meet a lot of people and talk to them and I see that they all have their own way of raising their frequency from the lowest point to the top of the hill. But does it last? Do many manage to get up every morning with this bright optimism and maintain it throughout the day? Let me answer my own question: No. Because underneath the surface, behind the cheerful facade, there is a reservoir of opposite emotions, the kind that pull us down. **To create a more stable reality, of joy and exaltation - we must engage more and more in internal cleansing and in the cultivation of self-love!** As in a garden of flowers - they will grow and thrive in a variety of attractive colors and shades only if gardening is done all the time! Do you agree with me? Self-awareness, like the gardening work, does not end. In the self-love wing too, it is necessary to tend - maintaining proper living conditions, nourishing, improving. Who will tend to you and take care of you? First of all you yourself.

"If I am not for myself, who will be for me?" This is a wise quote that should be adopted with great affection. It's not that I'm all alone, I have no one else and it's just me. Not that at all! But rather: I know best what is right or wrong for me, what lifts me up and what I need. And if I do not give it to myself - who's supposed to give it to me? Who **can** give it to me? It is quite obvious that no one will succeed in the mission like me.

Finally, another angle of behavior of a person who loves himself is the fact that **he enjoys helping others,** having clear knowledge that it is not at the expense of his own abundance. He is engaged in helping those around him with a sense of well-being and value and he enjoys sharing his material and moral wealth with others without expecting anything in return. A person with developed self-love does not deal with the question "What do I get out of it?" This question lessens the giving because people who receive something that is not given with a clean heart - feel it. Giving that is only in order to receive back is not joyful, and is not accepted with the same gratitude as is giving out of a genuine desire to help.

My dear, we are ending our meeting here. I explained to you as best as I could the importance and usefulness of developing self-love. I hope you decide to enroll in my course. If so, we'll meet again.

In the next course, on the virtues, you will learn the advancing qualities that you will strive to develop as a self-aware person. Lovely!

A big hug for the road!

Take care,

Miss Heart.

Exercises for Chapter 6:

1. In order to begin to **find out if you love yourself in the deepest and best possible way**, you can prepare yourself two lists: one list under the heading "I like in myself ..." and a second list under the heading "I do not like in myself ..." Take a few days to fill in the tables. Add features when you remember them. Your ultimate goal is to love yourself for all your properties and attributes and that means both lists! Even if you want to change some of the things you have written in them.

2. Sit down and think: **how do you show yourself love?** Put down the title: "To show love for myself I ..." and fill it with the things you do and the things you want and commit yourself to start doing. Use the chapter to get ideas for how you can show yourself love and add your own ideas.

Part 3

Features and Tools for Self-Awareness

Course 7

Virtues for a Smooth Ride

LECTURER: MS. SALLY VIRTUE
MASTER OF MERITS AND MANNERS

O h! Hello young lady.

Come in, come in, I'm waiting for you. I've prepared everything exactly according to the protocol, and you're supposed to relax into this meeting. Would you like a cup of coffee? A cup of tea? Please help yourself.

You have joined a workshop about cultivating virtues. They are very important in self-awareness, virtues. Believe me. What is beautiful about this is that you yourself will want to be an improved model of yourself as you progress in your studies. You will actually look for information and methods to help you become more and more virtuous. So, make yourself comfortable and I will begin.

Dear friend, what are virtues? A virtue is a trait and it has certain modes of thinking, emotions and behaviors that are derived from it. I would say that virtues are perceptions and behaviors that direct our attitude toward ourselves and the world.

These are perceptions and behaviors that guide us to a pleasant manner as we go about life, meaning constructive and non-destructive behavior. A code of conduct that promotes ourselves and others out of the understanding that there is enough space and resources for everyone.

Well, what are the virtues needed for a self-aware person? I'll list them and then I'll elaborate. Are you ready? Here they are: *generosity, gratitude, patience, courtesy and respect, tolerance, forgiveness, pride and modesty, compassion, assertiveness, courage, loyalty and the ability to trust.*

Generosity. A charming trait that makes the person who possesses it open-hearted and open-handed. A generous person gives others out of love and a sincere desire to help. This is wonderful, for it is unconditional giving without having to receive anything in return. Generous giving is not patronizing nor is it haughty conduct on the part of the giver who expects to be admired for his giving. **He who has developed self-awareness simply loves to help and is not busy thinking about the profit he will receive and what he "gets out of it."** He derives the satisfaction and pleasure from the giving itself, and therefore he gives and also receives. He is aware of the joy that giving makes him feel inside and that is his reward. The generous giver does not expect any reward, not even gratitude. However, if the thanks are given he is ready to receive them with a warm welcome. You know why? Because he understands the need of the recipient to give him something back - something to signal appreciation and gratitude.

And he does not reject the gratitude with embarrassment or self-righteousness. He rejoices in it and responds to it with light and love. That way, the giving of the generous person is a giving that leaves good taste for him, the giver, and for the other, the recipient.

Gratefulness. This is the other side of generosity. **The self-aware person also knows how to accept and is grateful for everything given to him. He accepts with joy, appreciation and thankfulness.** When he receives something from another person or from the universe, he does not feel ashamed, humiliated, weak or needy. Also, he does not think he owes a favor to the person who gave him - he knows that gratitude is the right response and that it balances the picture. Having received something will not open a debt here. Moreover, he knows that by being open to what is given to him, he himself gives back something because he allows the giver to feel the joy of giving. Do you understand, my dear? In receiving there is also giving. Think about it.

Patience. This is the next virtue that we will discuss and it is important, especially in places that are restless and stormy, where people have a hot temper. Maybe you know such places? The people there are always in a hurry, preoccupied with life's worries, highly impatient. One should learn to take a deep breath and strive for patience. It is important to be calm and cool, it is important to be moderate and restrained. The self-aware person senses when he is losing patience, when his temper is short and he knows how to relax. When he is calm, his responses are mild, restrained. The aware mind is inwardly attentive, and when something causes it to lose patience even a little - it is immediately aware of it. Something's wrong and patience must be summoned. **As a matter of fact, the skilled aware-person almost never loses patience, he is generally composed. He respects others enough** not to get mad at their slowness; he knows there is nowhere to hurry; he manages his time well and does not get stressed when things do not go according to plan.

A person who developed self-awareness understands that it is impossible for him to do everything according to his plan. After all, he does not live alone. Each step involves other people and circumstances, and it is worthwhile to trust the way things happen, to understand that there is a supreme wisdom that orchestrates and manages everything. Therefore, I will do my best to carry out my plan, but in the face of an obstacle or delay I will respond in moderation and serenity, not in anger, pressure or outburst. **The importance of this virtue cannot be overstated: patience enhances your health and helps you to conduct yourself in the world more easily and efficiently, with temperance and peace of mind.**

Courtesy and respect. You probably agree that a virtuous person is polite, good-mannered and respectful of himself and others. Right? Good. So no need to explain. But how does this relate to self-awareness? Well, my friend, let us remember that **self-awareness guides us to value ourselves and equally recognize the value of others.** The self-aware person perceives his fellow man not as a competitor but as equal and valuable! In addition, he knows how pleasant kindness is. The generous person can give another person the right of way, a polite response and generally treat him in a way that tells him: "I see you and cherish you, and I have no need to overcome you. You have enough time, resources and space and I have all that too. You are worthy and I am worthy, and everything is all right."

Tolerance. This attribute refers to accepting the other by agreeing that he can be different from me in his conduct, his appearance and his opinions - and that is fine. I do not need to argue with him, influence him or change him. **Tolerance is acceptance of others as is, without judgment and criticism**. I want to believe that in the aware person the degree of tolerance is very high. Just as he wishes to be himself, according to his nature and desires, according to his skills and opinions and according to the customs of the house and society from which he comes - so he allows any other person to be. Tolerance is a recognition of the right of everyone to live in their own way as long as they do not try to impose it on others.

By the way, you should know that tolerance is an advantageous measure for us, for accepting the other with ease ads to our health. Believe me. The peace and quiet that it contributes to us elongates our lives. On the other hand, fanaticism, criticism or racism shorten our lives - they consume energy, fatigue the heart, add wrinkles of anger and so on. Also, together with a measure of curiosity - tolerance allows us to learn new things from people around us. It lets us expand our world and include in it the customs of other communities: modes of clothing and appearances that we did not know before or music and art styles from other worlds. Thus, tolerance serves us in more than one way.

Forgiveness. The ability to forgive is a divine virtue, no less. In our course we will devote considerable time to the subject of forgiveness. Forgiveness for ourselves and forgiveness for others. Anyone who does not possess this quality or at least tries to develop it does an injustice first of all to himself. He holds grudges and he spends a lot of energy on maintaining the list of "Who did what to me, when, how and why." Can you see how exhausting this can be? It is unnecessary and not helpful. What's done is done and it is a shame to immerse oneself in bitterness over the past or in planning future revenge. The absence of forgiveness turns the person into a victim because he sees himself as being wronged or as someone who has fallen prey to a plot or an abomination. And you know what the most stupid thing about it is? That at least in some cases there was no intention of harming him and he was offended by the interpretation he himself gave to the events. In other words, the person who does not forgive hoards in his heart events some of which are the product of his imagination. And in any case - he pays a heavy price for keeping account of all the wrongs done to him. What does he get out of it? Only that he continues to bear the pain of the injury and there is no end to it.

I told you I meant self-forgiveness too. Because people tend to continue to be angry with themselves. They sink into guilt, regret and remorse, and again - what comes out of it? Nothing. Whatever happened - happened, you cannot go back and cancel it and the heavy load is not healthy. If we hurt someone - and we can still ask him for forgiveness - we should do it. Whether the other forgives us or not, it is important that we forgive ourselves, allowing that we acted out of our human weaknesses.

Can you understand how important it is to embrace the ability to forgive? Forgive yourself for mistakes and misdeeds, you cannot avoid them completely. Learn from your mistakes, try to improve your choices and assure yourself that in the future you will strive to act generously, thankfully, tolerantly and patiently. You will see that your mood is already improving, loads have fallen from your heart, and you will feel happier. Forgive yourself for everything you remember, release all self-beating, give up the pose of a victim. Set yourself free!

Forgive as much as you can others who hurt you. We will also work on this in my class. Of course in many cases it is not simple.

If you were wronged through sexual abuse, denial of rights, or any other mistreatment - it is hard to forgive. I am willing to say that some things **cannot** be forgiven, it is not possible. I will go so as far as to admit that there may be extreme situations that **should not** be forgiven. I am not the one to judge in all cases. But I beg you to try. Wherever you can include forgiveness in the picture, you will feel relieved. You will be kind first of all with yourself. And in our course, you'll be dealing primarily with yourself. **You will learn that cleaning up feelings of resentment, hatred, vengeance, anger, and traumatic memories will only do you good, and they are related to forgiveness, to yourself and to those who hurt you.**

Now look, my friend, we're talking about forgiveness for what has already been done. But forgiveness will always help us also in the present and in the future! With its help we interpret events, as soon as they happen, in a forgiving way, out of the understanding that perhaps the offender is not a person who has attained complete self-awareness, if there is such a thing at all. He is wrong in his behavior. He works with anxiety or defensiveness, and this is his story, not ours. We have a choice whether to take it in, take it to the heart, or let the matter pass by without leaving a scar. **From now on, we will refuse to hold grudges and judge harshly. Let mercy lessen the degree of judgment and increase the amount of forgiveness.**

Pride and modesty. Two virtues for the price of one. And no my friend, they are not opposites and do not contradict. As a matter of fact, they complement each other well! Together they are a priceless asset for the aware person: they shape and mold him and straighten his back, soften his face and add to it beauty. Because someone who is proud of himself and of his accomplishments, yet conducts himself modestly, is a person who lives in peace with his successes out of a sense of equality. Can you see that? Imagine how you will feel when you are proud of all that you are: of your history and your heritage, your deeds and accomplishments, your family of origin or the family you built and so on. You will walk with your head high up, happy with all the good you have, no matter what the environment thinks. You can always see what is beautiful and right in your life. But – keep your pride between you and yourself. There is no need to brag and boast. After all, as you have reasons to show off, everyone else has reasons to swell with pride. And that's wonderful! I wish we all enjoy ourselves and what life gives us. We will walk with joy and delight in our hearts, become generous and courteous, we will be happy for ourselves and happy for others. There is enough for all of us, and no one deserves more or less than the rest. So - pride and modesty. A winning combination.

Compassion. I suppose it is obvious why compassion is on the list of virtues. It is the opposite of evil, cruelty, and it contains a desire for the good of the other. We will dwell on it anyway, only to distinguish it from pity. **Compassion comes from a loving, forgiving, accepting and willing heart.** On the other hand, pity may be due to a sense of superiority, sometimes even accompanied by disrespect or contempt. If I feel pity for you - I may also be a little judgmental of you or at least consider myself to be in a better position than you. Pity belittles its object, don't you think so? We will, however, consider compassion as a measure that we want, a measure of self-awareness.

Again, as in the case of forgiveness, **we will also give compassion to ourselves**. We will be loving and tender to ourselves, and will do what is good, truthful, beneficial and healing for us. As we seek to be compassionate toward other people and indeed toward all living beings - so we seek it for ourselves as well. Let's fill our hearts with compassion.

Assertiveness. This means conducting oneself in a way that preserves ones' freedom of expression and all other rights, as well as those of other people. It also means protecting oneself without harming another. This includes the ability to say difficult things, when necessary, with composure and pleasantness. For example – being able to express anger in a constructive way without aggression or refusing someone firmly but politely. See? An assertive person does not need offensive words, shouts or dramas - he can arrange everything quietly, with self-confidence that cannot be ignored. He sets clear boundaries to others and does not allow them to do what harms, reduces, humiliates or limits him. His self-confidence signals to everyone he encounters: "Here is a person who respects himself and others and he expects the same from you." Assertiveness gives its' owner serenity and the knowledge that he can manage his affairs as much as possible without tensions and quarrels, and if he does find himself in such situations - he has ways to deal with them effectively and healthily.

In addition, the assertive person can ask for help and does not regard it as demeaning. Also, this person has independent opinions and expresses them without fear and in a respectable manner. He knows how to stand up for himself. You can see that it is certainly very worthwhile to nurture assertiveness as a leading virtue of the self-aware person.

Courage. Here, too, I wish to explain exactly what I mean. This is not about courage in battle, heroism of the kind that is related to fighting. It is the ability to act despite the fear that arises in a problematic situation. Such a situation requires finding the internal strength to do what is required in order to solve it. **The courageous person is aware of the fear and feels it, but he acts in spite of the fear because he has no desire to let fear control his life**. Those who are committed to self-awareness as a way of life know that it's okay to be afraid, in fact there is no one who is not afraid sometimes. And everyone is afraid of different things. The question is what he does with the fear.

So first of all it is recommended to feel the fear. Do not repress it, try to ignore it or pretend to be a hero who doesn't blink. We are not superman and we're not made of steel. So it's important that we admit to ourselves that we are afraid. If we have time to find out the origin of the fear - great. If not, we'll remember to take care of it later. As for now, we'll do what we can, and if we need help we'll ask for it. You do not have to deal with difficult situations alone, OK? So courage does not mean that we are fearless, but that we try to act with and despite the fear. But it does not end here. We said we would deal with fear later, when we had time. As students of self-awareness, we devote time to self-care and so it is very important and worthwhile to expose the source of the fear and try to remove it. You will learn in my course how to do it. We have our tricks, fortunately.

As we progress with the list of virtues you may notice that they are connected. It seems that if some of them are adopted - the rest come along ☺

Loyalty (first of all to yourself). We probably all agree on the importance of loyalty. A loyal person is perceived as honest, as one who will not betray you and will be at your side when necessary. Who doesn't appreciate loyalty, right? And in self-awareness we ask you to be faithful - first of all to yourself. What does that mean? It means sticking with your beliefs, even when that may be difficult for you; proceeding according to your inner feelings while repelling dictates from the outside; not succumbing to social pressure; meeting your own expectations of yourself and not those of others; being you - without trying to imitate someone else; taking care of yourself because you are important to you; standing behind your words; not folding in the face of criticism or opposition, as long as you know you are telling the truth and you want your opinion heard; and not denying yourself - your opinions, desires, aspirations and dreams.

Wow! That's very impressive, in my opinion. What do you think? Is it worth developing this virtue? By all means.

Trusting. The last virtue on the list. Why is trusting important and who exactly should we trust? First, it is important that we trust other people. Over-suspicion is a problem when we come to socialize, do business, gain the trust of others or have a relationship of love and even marriage. Trust requires an open heart that is not afraid to be hurt. And it's not that simple, is it? Because many of us have been hurt in the past, someone betrayed our trust, and now we want to protect ourselves from further harm. But it's not a good idea to go through life like that. **It is important to do self-awareness work to heal the wounds of the past, to develop mental strength and to open the heart again to friendship and love**. After all, most of our encounters with other people lead to fair, friendly, humane, positive interactions. Why get stuck with a broken and locked heart?

I want to expand the issue of trust. In my opinion, it is also worthwhile to develop trust in the process of life, in the way things flow, in how they all sum up well in the end. I highly recommend that you adopt a view that says: **The world is a safe place for me, things happen in my favor even if I do not always see it, it's all** for the better and everything happens just as it should. What do you say? Do you want to go through your days from now on confidently, putting your trust in the way your life-plot develops? Are you ready to drop the suspicion, the defensive perception, the fears and worries about what might or might not happen? I think it's worth it!

In conclusion, my dear, it is very important to understand one thing: the self-aware person is not perfect! But the whole list we went through now is of the virtues he is striving to develop more and more in himself. As we've said, he has compassion and forgiveness for himself, so when he fails or moves away from the virtues, he is not angry with himself. He tries to keep them as best as he can.

Right after this chapter you'll find exercises from me. I wish you enjoyable further reading and fruitful studies, and a lot of success. Cultivate the virtues whether you decide to commit to self-awareness or you continue deliberating. They'll always serve you well!

Sincerely,

Ms. Sally Virtue

Master of Merits and Manners

Exercises for Chapter 7:

In this chapter we described the virtues recommended for the self-aware person.

Learn them, think about each of them in your own context: to what extent do you have these qualities?

Think about how you can strengthen them and put them into your daily life.

- Generosity,
- Gratefulness,
- Patience,
- Courtesy and Respect,
- Tolerance,
- Forgiveness,
- Pride and Modesty,
- Compassion,
- Assertiveness,
- Courage,
- Loyalty,
- Trusting.

Course 8

Sports Class - Major Life Skills

LECTURER: MR. JOE WINNER
UNIVERSAL MULTIDISCIPLINARY CHAMPION

Hello Champion!

I'm very glad you came to practice. We, in the self-awareness circle, emphasize our connection with the body, but **we take the important things from the field of sports to the other areas of our lives**. OK. Are you ready?

I'm going to surprise you now, big time! In sports I first teach meditation! Surprised? I do not just teach to run and jump, in my class we do not only compete! I know that it is very important first of all **to relax, to release strain, to cool our engine, to relax muscles, to breathe deeply and to empty our minds**. That's my starting point and that's also the end point. Without it you cannot do anything. Do you understand? There is no sense in embarking on a journey that will require effort and a lot of energy when you are already tired by tension and lack of oxygen. And you know that's how you live most of the time! Pay attention, right now: your breathing is shallow... and your muscles are stressed ... your face is tense ... can you feel that? It's not good. Not good.

So come on, right now leave everything. Sit back, close your eyes, relax your body and take some slow, deep breaths. Come on, go ahead and do it! I'm waiting.

Very good. There is place for improvement and we will learn in depth how to meditate so as to really bring the body and mind to the zero point. It's so healthy, you have no idea! You'll fall in love with it. Our body recognizes good things and meditation is the best! I'll tell you something else - meditation teaches **concentration**. And every athlete wants to develop this capacity. Before he sets out, he wants to harness all his resources toward one goal - and that requires a lot of training, make no mistake! So meditation.

Let's go on. The next thing I teach you is **discipline**. You will learn how to train your **willpower** so that you can focus it on anything you decide to achieve. You can set yourself a goal and move on steadily, without giving in, without breaking, until you reach it! And this requires iron discipline. We will strengthen your willpower here until you don't recognize yourself. You will become a winner, a successful achiever, one who attacks the target and conquers it! Clear?

Moving on. The next topic we learn in sports lessons is jumping. All kinds of jumps – long jump, high jump, triple jump, and rope jump - all are relevant for us. Whatever you like. Because what's the point in jumping? That you always want to jump a little further, you're constantly striving to **get better**! And I'll teach you more than that - I'll teach you to make **quantum leaps**! You have no idea what you can do, dear lady! You do not even dream about the jumps and leaps I'm planning for you! And I suggest that you do not give up on this matter of jumping. If you don't practice and keep improving, I'm afraid you'll just stay behind. Anyone who does not invest does not progress. Clear?

Next. After jumping we learn to run. And I love long distances running. Listen: After the set off, which generates a huge burst of adrenalin, what happens? Many times we give it all at the beginning and then we run out of gas. We do not calculate correctly the size of our steps, our breathing and the energy needed - we burst out with all our strength and very quickly it just drains. We break down and quit the race. So I want to tell you that it's really a shame and this is not the right way to go about it - not on the running track and not on other tracks in life. We will learn to properly plan our conduct in order to spread our supplies wisely, because what is the purpose? To reach the end of the long runway. In the end there's something we want, something that will make us feel good when we get to it. Otherwise it's no use running there! And if I want to refine the point here, then what are we talking about? About **persistence**. Long distance running requires **the ability to move correctly over time and that is something that life demands from those who want to succeed**. Beautiful. Let's proceed.

Our next sport is archery. We'll learn it a bit differently than usual. Are you listening? We will learn to **set our own clear goals** before we start to shoot. Only then will we aim. And you know why? Because if you don't have clear goals, what will you aim at? I do not know. In my opinion, you will direct your arrows where you least want them to land. You'll find yourself shooting in the direction you do not intend. And why so? Because that's where you're looking! That's where your focus is! I want you to learn to set clear goals that will hold your attention and not let it be distracted in any direction. It's very, very important! Both in sports and in life - you will get to what preoccupies your thoughts and feelings. And I'm sorry to tell you that what concerns you most of the time is worries and qualms and fears. Right? In your head you run and re-run scenes of failures, accidents, tragedies, destitution and distress - whether they happened or not, whether they will happen or not! And when your mind is full of thoughts about what you do not want, where do you think you're headed? With no doubt, just toward those targets you do not want. OK? Understand? Great. Come on.

The next thing we work on in our lessons is **flexibility**. I really can't understand those who do not keep moving their joints on a regular basis, who do not preserve the ability to bend, fold, twist and turn their heads. Seriously. What is more important than a flexible body? This is what makes it possible to move freely, to pass through narrow openings, to look in all directions, to react correctly to any ball thrown at us or to any pit that surprises us on the way. And of course flexibility is important in life in general! I speak of the flexibility of thoughts, of emotions, of our actions on a daily basis. Yes? Because life surprises us all the time. What do you think? That it's going according to our plans? Much more not so than yes. How does the saying go? Man plans and God laughs. I'm not sure who says it but it fits here. It's very good to plan, these are the clear goals we talked about before. But I did not tell you that these goals sometimes somehow move, and at other times we come across a wall that springs up out of nowhere between us and the target, all kinds of weird things like that. You know? And then what do we do? Give up? We sit and cry and ask who moved our goal?

If we participated in sports lessons and we also perceived what we were taught there - then we probably have flexibility. That allows us to adapt quickly and respond to the change that has come to our attention. We find a way around the wall, sneak through the crack there, climb over or bend under the barrier and so on. **We do not break but adapt**. This is allowed only by our physical and mental flexibility. We get used to finding creative solutions, adjusting ourselves to the situation as it arises! That's cool, don't you think? Flexibility enables coping with changes, and changes are an integral part of life. We want to be flexible because otherwise we will become rigid and fixed, and not only will we not be able to react quickly and efficiently - but it will also hurt! The joints will be un-lubricated, rusty and motionless, and the brain will not be used to reacting quickly. And that's not good. Not good. So flexibility!

Excellent. Now swimming. From me you will learn two kinds of **swimming: with the current and against the current.** Very interesting. Note how it's also related to flexibility. Sometimes we have to go with what comes, where everyone goes and wherever life takes us - and not resist. We need to flow. The truth is that this is the easy part of swimming. You learned to move with the stream from the moment you were born. Be like everyone else, follow the herd, do what you're told, do not think too much. Adjust yourself to the norm. Right? Be normal. Terrific. That's how society loves you. But what if it does not suit you? If you suddenly manage to think independently and do not like what's happening? Maybe you notice that it's not convenient for you, not good for you, that's not who you are? What are you supposed to do, go on anyway? Go along with everyone, drift with the current even though you are miserable and want to go in another direction or another way?

So that's why I also teach you swimming against the tide, okay? Do not worry. I really don't think you should always do what everyone else does. And by the way, I also do not think you should always do what is convenient and easy. Obviously, it's easy to be a docile child who does what she's told. That way you will get caresses and the elders will be satisfied with you; you will fulfill your parents' fantasies and make them happy; you will not upset anyone, and you will fit into the school and workplace framework. So from my classes you will emerge an independent individual, and you will know how to go wherever you decide, even if it's a revolutionary route that you are not expected to take or it's upstream. You will be strong enough and practiced to swim confidently and courageously in your own way, even against the current. Good? Do we have a deal? Awesome. Next.

If you have to stop, do it. My pace is fast, you'll get used to it. Take some air, relax your muscles, and release stress. Smile. It's good for relaxing your face. When you are ready, we will continue.

The next profession I will teach you in sport lessons will be rope-walking. You think I'm laughing? No, I'm completely serious. Walking on a rope teaches you to **maintain balance**, and you really want to develop this ability, believe me. You want to know how to keep your balance when you're surprised - and life surprises all the time. You also want to know how to balance the things you burden yourself with - and that's something you do to yourself all the time. I'm really serious about balance lessons so that you do not crash, do not sway one way or the other. That may end badly.

What do we learn in rope-walking lessons? We learn how to maintain proper posture - straight back, face forward, hands spread out evenly; how to breathe in a regular and uniform way; how to bring our feet slowly one before the other on the rope; how to keep our eyes focused on one point without deviations; and finally - how to unite everything, because all parts of the body must bond and work together! Wow. I tell you - walking on rope is a fantastic profession, it is fabulous! If you control it, you will gain confidence that is priceless; you'll rely on yourself even when you have a hard time, when the bridge is very narrow or fragile, when you find yourself on an unpaved or bumpy road. You'll know you've been there already, you've done worse things: you've walked on a rope!!! So what's it for you, a narrow bridge or a crumbling road? You know what to do, you know how to hold yourself right and take one little step after another, out of well-earned balance and inner quiet.

Wait, I'm not finished yet. I teach you more than that: walking on a rope when you are loading yourself with equipment. Huh? What do you say? Some challenge! I ask you - where in life do you have to learn to balance what you are burdened with, that is, to put something on yourself - to see if it undermines you, to add something else - and to see what happens? When in life are you required to decide what to take with you and what not? How much to squeeze in - or what you're better off without? I'll give you a hint. Sometimes it's something you'll consider putting into your body, huh? Get it? I'm talking about balance in all areas of life - in food, drinking alcohol, smoking, workload, watching television, hanging out with friends, time alone with yourself. In any area you can think about. Balance is the name of the game - a little can be fine, but too much is often harmful. And how do we know when it's okay and when not? When we are balanced and when we get out of balance, endangering ourselves? We need to listen to the signals of the body and to our emotions and that too is part of learning to walk on a rope! OK?

Fine. Next we teach, in the Self-Awareness Department, sports that require playing in pairs. You can choose between table-tennis and court-tennis. One player against the other. There are also couple matches. You get it? It's not the same. But in both cases - singles or in pairs - it is important to learn how to interact with another person. After all, we do not live alone, we interact with other people large part of the time, and it is important to know how to deal with one another when competing as well as when cooperating. OK? We practice tennis to **develop our interpersonal skills**! What does that mean? We learn to win and we learn to lose; we learn to predict the actions of the other and to respond or make them act differently; we learn to play out of respect for ourselves and respect for our opponent or partner; we develop the ability to compete in order to win, and in other cases we develop the ability to combine effort with another person and to share the success.

All this is so important because we want to play the game of life with fun and pleasure, having just and respectful human relations. We want to maintain social and professional ties that will advance us, serve us and allow us to participate in healthy interpersonal dynamics. You may be a bit confused because I talked about pair games, but the above is true for group games too! We need to develop these abilities for good conduct in groups where we are members: family and social groups or work teams! You're right.

That is why we will also learn soccer, basketball and other team games. It is important to learn how to take your place within a group and at the same time leave room for other members as well; how to be one of the team without losing your uniqueness; how to contribute as part of the joint activity and how to keep the rules out of self-respect and respect for others. You see, we want to know how to fit into the team, to play our part and to advance without stepping on others. We want to succeed by of our appropriate actions and not at the expense of someone else.

All of this is important whether you are a player in the group or you are its coach or manager, right? In the end it's the same thing - a matter of team play and mutual respect. You want to fulfill your role in maximum ability and success, alongside and in combination with parallel or complementary role-players. After all, together is best. We are all one human tissue! But I'm getting carried away. Excuse me. Where were we? Ball games. **Developing group skills**. Great. We're almost done.

The last sport you will encounter in the course is bungee jumping. Totally true. By the time we get there you'll be ready for it, trust me. You will have all the necessary skills and tools. What are you practicing in bungee jumping? The ability to be hanging between heaven and earth without losing your poise! The ability to cope when life throws you from high up into the dark, and you're terrified. When you must **agree to lose control** and rely on the rope that holds you and is your only connection to life. This is the highlight of the course. You will jump into the abyss; experience a fear like you have never experienced before; agree of your own free will to be thrown into the unknown; take a huge gamble and put full and blind trust in whoever operates the facility. What do you say champion? Can you see what we're talking about here? It's crazy. And this is the summit of abilities that we need to develop for a life of self-awareness: **the courage to release**!

Well, after I've told you all about the sports we've got, I want to say something in general. We, in our department, look at each student as a private case, as a unique individual. So we will teach you to **measure your progress in relation to yourself** and not in comparison to others. Even when there are competitions - you will want to keep achieving better results but you will learn not to panic if you do not win. **The important thing is to do your best and improve all the time**. We put emphasis on developing your personal style that takes advantage of your skills and strong qualities. You will develop your own way of doing things and dealing with difficulties. Is that clear?

Beautiful. Now, as I explained, we do some meditation before we part. Lean back ... straight spine... close your eyes ... breathe deeply and relax your muscles. Rest for a few minutes and we will surely meet again.

I foresee victories for you!

Mr. Joe Winner

Universal Multidisciplinary Champion

Exercise for Chapter 8:

Read again all the characteristics and skills that the different sports disciplines mentioned in the chapter develop, and think about them:

1. Which of them do you have and to what extent?

2. In what way can they be expressed in the different areas of your life?

3. How can you improve these features in yourself?

Course 9

About Wasting and Preserving Personal Energy

LECTURER: MS. HONEY BELLE
SENIOR DIRECTOR OF HUMAN RESOURCES

Hello there!

I'm really glad to see you. You, who is considering enrollment! I have no greater happiness than to see those engaged in such considerations. What could be better? So come in, I'll give you more food for thought. And I'll tell you the truth: I hope to be the one who will convince you!

I teach energy conservation or how to manage our personal energy supply, our individual resources. We talk about resources like physical strength, time, money, skills and talents. These valuables are mostly taken for granted, as something we just have. We use them as if there is no tomorrow, squandering them thoughtlessly. Does that make sense to you? I love to laugh and if it was not so sad I would literally burst out roaring with laughter. What is that! Whoever heard of the waste of precious resources on the one hand and the limiting of free resources on the other? Because if you think about it, you will see that we squander time, energy and money - and we are miserly about breathing or the expression of our inborn talents. It is precisely there that we are suddenly very reserved. Why? I want you to learn how to take advantage of what is free and expand it, and to use in a calculated and economical manner what is costly or scarce. My goal is, for example, that you keep your strength so that you'll be energetic, instead of so tired and exhausted.

The thing is that most people's behavior, including that of beginners in self-awareness, is one that allows their energy to leak without it being noticed. They apply their energy when it's unnecessary - and I'll tell you where, shortly. When do they finally pay attention to the leak? When there's a problem! And especially when the problem is already big! A health problem, a financial problem, time pressure and things like that. There are all kinds of mechanisms that call attention when there is a serious disruption in the energy field, and that's a good thing. But we want to learn to avoid the problems, to understand how to behave correctly and to manage our lives wisely. And that's why I'm here. I know how to run things so well that you really want to study with me! If I did not exist - they would have to invent me! Well, I'm kidding, of course. I told you I like to laugh ☺

In my opinion, laughter is very good for your health and for a good life. And when do we laugh? When we're happy. When are we happy? When we're not sad, we're not worried and we're not tired. Correct? So that is what it's all about. **Come and learn** how to be not only happy but actually blissful. And learn how to keep the strength and resources available to you, how to utilize them to maximum efficiency and with minimal waste of energy. Do you get the idea? Still not convinced? Well, then I have to continue the lecture. I'll explain more about what I mean and you'll see that it's not complicated and that it really matters. You will understand how much you ought to learn to manage your personal resources.

Let's start with physical energy. **We lose energy when we are tense for no reason** and it happens a lot. Unlike the wild animals, we got used to being tense all the time, as if we were living in a jungle full of evil animals ambushing us. Now look, I can understand that - sometimes the city is really a jungle! And sometimes the motorway is like a race track! Man to man is sometimes a hungry wolf. Our lives are not calm. So no wonder we got used to being alert all the time. If you pay attention, you'll see that your whole body, including your face, is constantly tense. Your muscles are almost never completely slack and relaxed.

You experience an energy of attack and danger **also through the media**. There are quite a few places in the world where cruelty and evil are second nature. A person relaxes in the living room in front of the television - watching the news - and what bursts out of the screen? Corruption, ugly politics, violence of all kinds, natural disasters and man-made catastrophes, car accidents, wars - it's just shocking. And his body responds to all that! The same thing when trying to read a newspaper. I'm not surprised people escape to the gossip columns. Even the sports section is not really an island of peace, is it?

As a result of all the harsh information and sights that enter our system, the body decides that there is a need to prepare for an attack and that it must be on the defensive - and never cease! This requires enrolment of all structures in favor of the matter. Emergency recruitment. And this exhausts us. Do you understand, my friend? What we need to do is to train ourselves to rest more, to behave pleasantly and easily, not to run and rush when there is no need, and to greatly reduce our news consumption through all the channels in which they are published.

More about the body: learn to eat healthy food, avoid smoking and **start listening to what the body tells you and what it asks you to do**. Your body keeps telling you what makes it feel good and what does not; what foods are right for it and what are not; when it is hungry and when it is thirsty and so on. It keeps signaling you - but you cannot decipher the clues! So you eat what experts tell you to eat, you read articles and hear lectures, and you're pretty sure you know what's healthy. But the fact that you hear, does not necessarily mean you do what they say. And of course what they say is not necessarily true for every person or specifically for you! Now, when you eat things that are not good for you, not in the correct amount or not at the right timing - what do you think happens to your body? It strives, it does a lot of unnecessary work that takes away its energy and then you get tired. If you continue to treat your body senselessly and with carelessness it may reach a breaking point. At breaking points diseases break out, muscles weaken, bones become depleted, cells begin to err and alter their functions and the situation deteriorates. And that's all because you do not manage your diet properly, as well as the times of activity and rest or what you ingest through your five senses!

There are other ways in which you lose precious energy. Like when you think **unpleasant thoughts**. Thoughts of criticism, resentment, worry. Running episodes from the past or the future repeatedly like a broken camera or a clip running in your head in an endless loop. Do you agree with me? Negative thoughts are very bad for us. They steal our energy, empty and weaken us and violate the delicate balance of our body and mind systems.

And what about friends? Do you have **friends who suck your energy**? That after meeting them you are sad, upset or just exhausted? Think about them and think of the friends who lift you up, that every meeting with them fills you with joy and adrenalin! You can understand the obvious conclusion. Take care of yourself, remember that you are loved and precious and decide that you want to surround yourself only with supportive and encouraging people who radiate love and goodwill to you. Be picky about the people you spend your time with.

And this brings us to the next issue - time. That is also a resource of ours! And we spend it almost criminally. There is a time for everything - even to do nothing. It is okay since we should also rest. So when are we **wasting time**? When we do things in an inefficient way or not at the right time, when we do not use the time well and do not fill it with things that contribute to us. I imagine you'd like to know what the ideal time management is. Am I right? Well, when treating time as a resource to be respected, a person plans his day. He allocates time for activity and work, time for pleasure and leisure and time for sleep and rest. Think about yourself for a moment. You have to include in your weekly schedule: work, school, sports, meetings with friends, family engagement, chores and errands, cleaning and shopping and also, presumably, breaks for rest and renewal. You want to do everything at the right time, not too late and not out of reception hours. If you don't check in advance and plan correctly, you will find yourself in a rush because you did not set out on time, and in other cases you will have to wait for your turn or come back again at a more appropriate time. Either way - it is a waste of energy due to lack of accurate timing.

Another way to lose energy due to disrespect for the time resource is thru **procrastination**. When we do not do things on time it often has unpleasant consequences that cause us pressure and worry or even cost us fines and penalties.

Money is undoubtedly a precious resource for human beings. Let's talk about the **waste of money**. Actually, we do not have to talk about it - I guess you know where this energy goes. You know when you spend money without justification and at the expense of more important things. In fact, what robs our mental energy is the **lack** of money. When money slips through our fingers and via the credit card without us being sufficiently aware of it, most likely that when the time come for us to pay bills, buy food and the like – we don't have enough money left. Then we pay with the resources of the soul, in the form of insomnia, worries and looking for ways to close the gap. Do you know, my friend, that rich people also compare prices, check the practicality of acquisitions, plan expenses? We need to know where our money comes from and where it goes so as to keep our peace of mind and live a good life.

You could say that, in general, any **disorder** in the different areas of our life costs us wasted energy. I claim that a neat room, an organized working table, planned lessons – are all very important. This is the right way to live if we want peace and order within our inner world. The inner reflection of the external order is expressed in tranquility and in orderly and efficient thinking. This order - internal and external - saves our strength, time and sometimes money. It saves us energy.

To summarize the subject so far: unbalanced eating, energy-consuming contacts, clutter and disorder, lack of planning, debts not paid on time, procrastination of things, mismanagement of money - all these create worry and unnecessary leakage of energy. OK?

Can you imagine that I have not finished yet? There are other ways we all lose energy unnecessarily! For example - **work can deplete us** if it does not suit us, if we do not enjoy doing it. When a person goes each morning to spend many hours in a place he does not want to go to - obviously he pays a very high price in his body and soul resources, right? A job that is wearing us down, that is not enjoyable, is unfulfilling or is not properly rewarded - may cost us a very high price, even to the point where we develop conditions of illness and depression. Yet, many people compromise about their work. After all, one has to earn a living and it is not always easy to find a new and better job. So they ignore the warning signs of the mind and the body; they tell themselves stories and justify the fear of getting up and leaving with all kinds of excuses and arguments. They hang on to a place that is not good for them, too afraid to attempt change.

Let's continue. For many people, **home is not a safe and peaceful place**, it is not a refuge from the hardships of life. For these people, their house is a place where their energy is stolen because a member of the household treats them in a diminishing, criticizing, dismissive and offensive manner - all the time. They have no rest. Can you imagine how exhausting it is to live in a house like this? Your own home!

OK. In my opinion, we examined enough energy loss options. **So now is the time to give a picture of a healthy life, a life of**

efficient and beneficial usage of the resources available to human beings.

If you want to create for yourself such a healthy life, you will probably insist on **a diet that is right for you**, with balanced dosages of the nutrients and with sensible quantities. It will be a varied diet that will please and satisfy you without burdening the body and overloading the digestive system. You will also engage in some kind of **sports activity** that will be enjoyable and will exercise and strengthen your body. The physical workout will have beneficial consequences also on the mental level. It will uplift and delight you.

I believe that you will make sure that you **use your time well** and that you will be able to assign reasonable portions of it to study, work, tasks, recreation and rest. You will develop your skills! Because I did not tell you, but even boredom can wear you out, while **using your talents and skills for creation and pleasure** will charge you with amazing energy! This will happen also when you spend time with people who are pleasant to you, with whom you have a relationship of appreciation, respect and love. When you fill the day with interesting occupations and positive people - you will find that you are alert, happy and full of energy.

I hope you will also remember to **breathe**, to take large doses of air, preferably clean air. At least once in a while. And there is one last thing I want us to dwell on a bit. Another way to recharge ourselves and fill with energy. I mean the flow of abundance through **giving and receiving**. This is also an aspect of managing our personal energy. An imbalance between accepting and giving may disrupt us. Giving without retribution will empty us, while those who only accept or take and do not know how to give - I think they will just be all alone at the end. Also, they will miss the joy of giving. When you know how to give in the right way and how to receive in the right way, and there is such a thing as the right way to give and take - you will find it is a very enjoyable way to let abundance flow. The universe likes to fill vacancies so if you give - you make room for something to replace what you gave, fill the place you emptied. If you do not give to others and keep it all to yourself, I'm afraid you'll get stuck with too much, create an energy blockage and the universe will not be quick to give you things. Can you see that? It seems to me a most natural thing that we should want to give, yet it is very important that we maintain a balance between giving and receiving, that we do not neglect either.

By the way, I mean any form of giving - clothes and things we no longer need, gifts, attention, lending an ear or a hand, hugs and smiles, anything! Giving is meant to benefit others. When we know how to give - it does not only benefit others but also ourselves. It makes us happy. And so is the correct acceptance - it is the acceptance of everything that another person wants to give us with gratitude, with pleasure and with an open heart. Such a receiving also envelopes in it giving, right? It delights the giver, he enjoys his gift being accepted so gladly.

How do we end? Perhaps by reminding ourselves simply to **notice what tires us and what fills us with strength**. We should try to avoid worries, debts and disorder. We may bring into life order and planning, enjoyable occupations, and people who are pleasant to be with. We will learn to find the light and the easy, the efficient and the useful, the simple and the clear. **Simplicity and clarity** are wonderful words that I recommend you adopt. And finally - try to be happy. **Happiness is very much a matter of choice**. Think about it.

That's it dear, as far as I'm concerned you are dismissed.

I wish you good energies!

Ms. Honey Belle

Senior Director of Human Resources.

Exercises for Chapter 9:

1. Practice regular muscle release and facial relaxation. Constant tension of the body tires it.

2. Pay attention to what causes you stress. Try to reduce those stressors in your life, most of them are not necessary.

3. Consider ways of limiting news consumption through the different means of the media. You will lower loss of energy due to the negative frequency they are mostly charged with. Avoiding the news updates and other stressing programs will improve your feeling and will give you time for fun and rewarding activities.

4. Take responsibility for your health. Put order into your diet and exercise plan and listen to what your body asks you to do.

5. Monitor your thoughts: exchange unpleasant thoughts with positive and empowering ones.

6. Choose your friends carefully. Spend your time in a sympathetic and empowering company.

7. Manage your time wisely. Plan activities in a time log. Do not postpone doing things, rather divide and spread out tasks so that it's easy to do them on time.

8. Take the time to manage your money - expenses versus income. If necessary seek professional help.

9. Arrange your home and office! Disorganized surroundings sap your energy.

10. Do you like your job? Does it refill or deplete your energy? Make sure to work in a place that has positive energies and in a role that suits you.

11. Out of love for yourself, do not let anyone hurt you inside your home. The house you live in should be your sanctuary, your safe and calm refuge. If this is not the case, it is worthwhile to do what is necessary to change the situation, even by seeking help from an external source.

12. Do your best to give and receive with a loving heart and in a balanced way.

Course 10

Self-Help Methods – A First-Aid Kit

LECTURER: MR. S.O. HELP
A FIRST-AID SPECIALIST

Dear Friend,

Nice to meet you!

I am aware that most people, upon feeling the slightest pain - physical or mental - run to the medicine cabinet. Feeling a sharper ache - they call an ambulance or at least go to the doctor. I hope you are not among those. I want to influence you to adopt advanced yet simple self-help techniques, so that in an emergency, you will have tools of self-calming therapy and of gentle, healing energies. The purpose of these is to allow the body to awake the healing powers it naturally has. As you know, self-awareness studies intend to help a person help himself.

I would like to say that I do not dismiss the importance of receiving outside help. It is unreasonable to ask that a person refrain from receiving treatment from another person, more skilled or less skilled, whose intentions are good. But it would be best if we were all trained in self-help.

In this course we are going to teach you how you can instantly calm your agitation; release the body from the chains of suffocating and constraining panic; memorize words that will direct your imaginative power to healing; and activate techniques that will immerse you in energies of light and love. And I must emphasize to you, here and now, that there is no greater healing power than love! So I suggest that you work on that: learn to love yourself fully. As you've already discovered, we have an excellent course on this subject.

The initial help for any situation in general, and the state of unpleasantness or an accident in particular is: breathe! And it turns out that even this simple action I have to teach. It is true that every baby, right after coming into the world, begins to breathe. And it is to be hoped that he doesn't stop until his dying day, yes? But if you pay attention to your breathing, for example now, you will easily notice how superficial and shallow it is. Makes you want to take great gulps of air, fill your lungs, right? For some reason we constantly limit our breath. This is unnecessary. I understand that in times of danger or panic our breath shortens, this happens along with other stress reactions. But most of the time we can afford to breathe comfortably and generously yet we turn down this option! Instead we prefer to hold back and use only part of the lung capacity. That may be enough for us to continue to live and even function but we can improve our function by deepening our breathing. I'm sure our brain will be happy to get more oxygen, and the rest of the body too. What do you think?

So especially when you need first aid - it's important that your body knows how to control your breathing. It is therefore necessary to **practice deep, relaxed breathing on a regular basis until it becomes a habit** and will be available to us in times of trouble. It is precisely when we are in distress that our long, full breath can contribute to our relaxation. In addition, it will set a flow of oxygen to the stressed heart, the muscles and the vital organs that are working more intensively. So make it a habit to pause during the day and just breathe slowly, filling your lungs. Luckily, we get used to good things quickly. The body will begin to ask for the right breathing, will demand more air. And when you are pressed, as a first aid, your full breath will be an available and familiar support.

The second thing you should have in the first aid basket that you carry with you everywhere is the ability to **relax your muscles, your whole body**. That's because the body is quick to respond to the signs of danger by stiffening, by entering a state of readiness and alertness. You've probably heard of fight-flight-freeze reactions. This is a variety of possible responses in the event of a threat to our security. All of these reactions involve the muscular system. That's why I suggest you learn to relax your muscles. Whenever you have a moment to take care of yourself, inhale deeply and ease your body.

What else can you do to help yourself in a crisis? You can, of course, **say to yourself soothing words**. After all, that's exactly what any other person would do if they were with you. They would try to reassure you with warm words that show support, love and positive thinking. The problem is that if you are under pressure, maybe in panic, you do not think clearly, you are frightened and how will the right words come to you? Of course it would be nice if you were not alone at that moment, if there was someone compassionate with you who was not as nervous as you, and he would find the words that would activate your relaxation button. But if there is no such person next to you, or there is someone else who's also nervous, you should have a familiar sentence that you can easily summon or that will, better yet, pop up automatically. Prepare in advance some **soothing mantras** such as: "All is well, God is with me"; "Love and light surround me and give me protection"; "Healing energy is flowing into me"; "Peace and tranquility. Everything always happens for the best"; "Any obstacle is for my higher benefit" or any other sentence. The main thing is that you interpret this mantra as reassuring.

Pack these three elements - deep breathing, relaxing your body and saying a mantra that gives you self-control. Learn to do all three together, so that when there is a need they will be retrieved effortlessly. At the hour of test you will not be able to think of the right words, so you must prepare them in advance. Believe me, it is important to practice and teach the body **an automatic response of composure and self-control.**

In the case of real danger, after these first measures it is important to call for help. At this point you will be able to think more clearly about how to do it, and when you contact helpers you will be able to explain better, without panic, where you are and what you need. Even when you are not in danger, but you do need support - contact and summon a family member, a close neighbor, a good friend - whoever can encourage and help. It is definitely recommend that you **ask for help.**

Prayer is also a request for help: we place our trust in God and draw comfort and strength from Him. It is always possible to ask for help and guidance from a supreme source that we believe in. It is amazing every time anew how faith can help in times of crisis. Those who turn to such help receive it immediately and it is worthwhile learning to identify it. We will talk to you more about this in the following courses, and tell you about the possibility of receiving help and energy treatment from the spiritual guides that accompany you. In this case, you use external help that is always and everywhere within your reach. You just have to ask for it.

There are other ways to help ourselves at a time of difficulty. For example - it always helps to **hug a tree**. Have you ever tried? Also embracing a beloved and familiar animal can encourage us immediately and surely. If you think about it, every hug helps! Hugging someone else and even hugging yourself, as strange as it may sound.

In addition to all the tools I have mentioned, you can also enlist **guided imagery** to remind your body that it can repair itself. Our body is smart and it has the wonderful ability to restore itself: wounds heal like magic, the immune system sends soldiers to beat bacteria of various diseases and there is a constant turnover and renewal of all our cells. This is simply amazing! And with the help of imagination we can speed up our curing and healing processes. Meditation to insert light and love into all organs; meditation in which we imagine how a tumor disappears or how a damaged organ returns to function fully; and the screening of an inner film of ourselves in perfect health and happiness. All of these can support the body and help it when we need healing. I wrote down for you, in the exercises attached to this chapter, a reminder to practice guided imagery so that you would know how to use it when necessary.

If possible, you can boost your spirits through **music, movement, and dance**. As a first aid this is great since it allows you to raise your frequency so that you have more power to deal with the situation. It's not **in place** of dealing with it, but just so that **you'll be able** to do it.

I also suggest that you learn a healing method that enables self-treatment. The method I teach and use myself is **Reiki**. This is a kind of healing, that is: transferring energy from outside to my palms. I let in life energy through my Crown Chakra down into my head. It comes in and flows through my body and into my hands. My palms warm up and I can put them where I feel the need. If, say, my stomach aches - I put my hands on it and feel the heat sink in and soothe. This is outstanding! Since learning Reiki, many years ago, I am grateful for being able to take care of myself at any opportunity and any place, without the need for tools or supplies. I just ask for Reiki in my heart, feel a pleasant tickle in my scalp, my hands warm up and here I am ready to take care of myself. And of anyone else, of course ☺

Come to learn Reiki with us, **or find yourself another method of self-care** and learn it. This will give you a tremendous degree of freedom in life. Reiki helps me deal with the ailments of the body but also with the distress of the soul. The Reiki energy is intelligent and loving, it will never hurt me and I can always connect to it when I need help: when it hurts, when I feel ill, when I'm not calm or when my mood is low. I put Reiki hands on myself, calm down and then I can find out for myself what is going on and what else is right for me to do.

The last method I offer you today to provide yourself with first aid is **giving thanks**. Be thankful for everything you have. When you feel self-pity; when your mood is low; when you do not see the light at the end of the tunnel or when you are in physical pain or a pain of the heart – then it is just the right time to say thanks. In times of distress - start counting all the good things in your life and say thanks for all your blessings. Say, and also **feel** thankful! It may seem that thanking while you are in a bad state is the most unreasonable thing to do, because after all, what exactly is there to thank about? You're focused now on what's really wrong with your life! But that's exactly the idea: **reversing your point of view and putting the situation in the right perspective.**

When you list the things for which you can thank, you see that it is a very long list! Compared to it, the less successful moment you are experiencing now loses its power and importance, it is dwarfed by all the good you have. Isn't it? Besides, giving thanks brings you more things to thank for, and of course that's welcome. More of the good stuff will tilt the scales further in the right direction and the lesser times will occupy a diminishing part of your reality. See?

So here I have equipped you with a first aid kit that goes with you everywhere.

Take care of yourself and be well,

Mr. S.O. Help

A First Aid Specialist.

Exercises for Chapter 10:

1. **Prepare yourself a first aid kit**: Practice **slow and full breathing + muscle relaxation + a mantra!**

2. Learn a self-care method such as **Reiki.**

3. **Hug** many trees, animals and humans. It also helps as first aid in a crisis.

4. Practice **guided imagery** to remind your body of its healing ability.

Summary

Here we have come to the end of this book, in which you were presented with the focal points of the courses taught at the Department of Practical and Spiritual Self-Awareness. I appreciate the fact that you invested in yourself and took the time to read and learn in order to bring self-awareness into your life. You probably understand the tremendous importance of your decision to take charge of your life and make it a good and satisfying one!

What have we learned in the pages of the book?

Right at the beginning I made clear to you what you should expect if you decided to commit yourself to walking the path of self-awareness from now on. I told you that everything you learn in our department will be for your own use, since you have no right to change anyone except yourself. I also told you that choosing awareness as a way of life is very rewarding but it does not guarantee that everything will be pleasant and easy. Do you remember? You will have to be prepared to deal with heavy material and with difficult feelings that will arise while you deepen your self-awareness. Also, you will be required to give up your self-importance, you can expect periods of loneliness during your transformation and not all your friends and acquaintances will applaud you for the wonderful progress you make.

At the end of my presentation I asked you to **remember that you were perfect and wonderful just as you are, here and now**, and I urged you to also remember to take breaks in your self-study and to include times when you could **just be**.

Then we went on to review all the courses and each of lecturer presented their course to you personally.

In the presentation of the first course the honorable Mr. Sigfroid Young sketched the structure of the human soul as he understands it and in a way that would serve you in your self-awareness work. You have learned that **the soul consists of four parts: the Overt, the Covert, the Social and the Spiritual.** Mr. Young also characterized the self-aware student's desired characteristics such as curiosity, open mindedness, perseverance, independence, the ability to take rest breaks and a recognition of his own uniqueness.

Our second course was introduced by our talented lecturer Mrs. Holly Day who presented **the connection between the body, the soul and the spirit** - that is, how the body, soul and spirit of a person work together. The picture was complemented by detailing the **seven main chakras**, which relate to each of the different spheres of life. Thus, you have expanded your understanding of the structure and the conduct of the whole being called "man".

The third course you encountered in this book deals with the source and purpose of the spirits. The lecturer, Mr. Joshua of Galilei, explained to you **how human spirits were created and what they do during the course of life**. In their numerous incarnations they manifest themselves in human bodies and undertake, each time, different experiences, improvements and lessons.

The fourth course, given by Ms. Joy Little, is about **the influence of childhood and our inner child**. I hope you now understand how patterns of thought, emotion and behavior are created when we are children and that they do not always serve us well as we grow up. The wounds that still hurt us must be healed. The inner child who lives within us and in many ways controls us needs to be given some loving care and we must form a good relationship between the child part and the adult part - both of whom are us.

Lecturer Mr. A. Smart offered an overview of course number five, which deals with **self-esteem and self-acceptance**. He emphasized how much you need to know yourself better and to accept without criticism who you are including all your parts and facets. You have learned that it is good for us to be at peace with ourselves and to be comfortable with who we are, even if there are things that we want to change in ourselves.

Course number six was presented to you by the expert Miss Heart, who spoke to you about the need to learn to **love yourself unconditionally.** It was explained to you that when you love yourself you will take care of yourself and will not agree to stay where you are not happy or well. Additionally, your environment will be more loving towards you, your self-confidence will rise and you will be healthier, physically and mentally. Self-love will allow you to strive for a life of joy and self-realization.

In course number seven we learned about the virtues, the qualities and patterns that advance us and greatly improve our lives. These qualities characterize the self-aware person and they are: **generosity, gratitude, patience, courtesy and respect, tolerance, forgiveness, pride and modesty, compassion, assertiveness, courage, loyalty, and the ability to trust.** The course's teacher, Ms. Sally Virtue, explained to you in detail how beneficial these virtues are for the quality of life of the self-aware person. They color his behavior in shades that are calm and relaxed and they help him overcome the potholes of life in a more easy and advantageous manner.

The eighth course was presented by our wonderful athlete, Mr. Joe Winner, who presented you with sports that you should specialize in as best you can, in order to succeed in your self-awareness life. Those sports aim to develop in the student useful skills such as: the ability to relax and concentrate, will power, perseverance, flexibility and much more.

In chapter nine you met another of our wonderful lecturer, Ms. Honey Belle, who explained to you about the **waste and preservation of your personal energy**. You learned that there are various types of energy resources available to men - such as his body and soul strength, time and money. He can manage all of them wisely so that they will not leak until he is weakened and has gone out of physical, mental or practical balance.

Finally you came to the last chapter of this book, chapter ten, where you learned from the lecturer, Mr. S.O. Help, methods of first aid and self-help! This is a personal toolbox that goes with you everywhere and is available to you in moments of need.

And now, my dear, I remind you that most of the chapters have exercises attached to them so as to anchor their ideas in the reality of your life. Did you practice them?

If not, I strongly recommend that you go back to the beginning of the book and devote a few days to some serious practice. I cannot overstate the importance of applied practice of these proposed exercises. Only their implementation will begin to show you how self-awareness work improves life. Try - and see for yourself!

And if you did practice the exercises - excellent! Good for you! You can go back and practice them again from time to time. I believe you already see their usefulness and the significant improvement they have made in your life.

What's next?

I warmly invite you to read book #2: "Freedom, Abundance and Fulfillment". It is a direct continuation of the guide you have just read for it unfolds ten more wonderful courses we teach in our department! The book adds valuable knowledge and tools for continuing your journey. It is highly recommended!

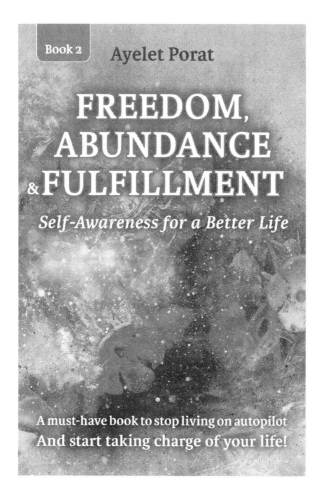

Take care and all the best,

Always at your service,

Ayelet Porat.

To purchase the second book or to get in touch with me and keep up to date on my future books

Visit my official Author Page on Amazon

Printed in Great Britain
by Amazon

55904741R00085